TODDLERS' DISCIPLINE

A SURVIVAL GUIDE TO TOT(S)' GROWTH SPURTS. GUILT-FREE MINDFUL PARENTING METHODS TO TAME TANTRUMS, ESTABLISH RESPECT AND HAVE TODDLERS THAT LISTEN IN A POSITIVE NO DRAMA HOME

Nicola Davies

MINDFUL PARENT Academy

Table of Contents

Preface

This book is part of a series of manuscripts from the Mindful Parent Academy. This growing collection contains books that tackle various aspects of the lives of modern parents with its inevitable challenges and unfathomable joys. All our books are driven by a compassionate, non-judgmental, and positive approach that aims to support parents in their journey into parenthood. Our mission is to build a world that gives back to family its core role as the foundational institution that sustains society and that provides wellbeing for all its members. Our revolution starts here and now. And it starts with You. It starts by wanting to, and being capable of, empathically looking after our thriving little people that constitute the future of our human society. This starts by equipping parents with the right knowledge and activities when it comes to strategically thinking about your toddler's development. At the heart of the Mindful Parent Academy there is a mission that is to shift the current trend that sees parents either feeling guilty and worried for spending too much time with their children to the detriment of their career or personal development. Or vice versa, a world where parents cannot spend enough time with their kids because of the strains put on them by their adult life and their job commitments. At the Mindful Parent Academy, we believe that any parent around the world should be put in favourable conditions in order to enjoy the right to be fully involved in this wonderful period of their child's life while being supported by the larger society. It is not a coincidence that in any given culture, in any part of the world, family (whoever this includes) is what drives people's actions, interests and passions. Stressed by the demands of modern life, sleep deprived and physically exhausted, modern parents can find it very difficult and challenging to deal with normal toddler's developmental growth spurts. In fact, it is quite normal and should be expected that in order to grow, toddlers will go through cycles of sleep disturbance, irritability, stubbornness, misbehaviour, tantrums and even meltdowns. Unprepared and unequipped with the right tools, parents can feel adrift and end up over-reacting, raising their voices or even misusing their words with their little people. This inevitably starts a cycle of guilt and despair that will inevitably spiral down with time. Your child and your mental health and your whole family's welfare are at stake here. However, at the Mindful Parent Academy we believe that everyone can build a no drama home full of giggles, loud laughter and singing kids. A place where a sense of harmony and stability reigns, no matter what. With this intention in mind, you need to embark on a personal mission to reach and maintain a mindful balance. We believe that there cannot be a flourishing tree without sturdy roots and that 'you cannot pour from an empty cup'. Therefore, whatever are your circumstances, No Matter What, we support the idea that you must first look after your own mental, physical, and spiritual well-being. And without guilt. We want you to first reflect on the experiences that you had as child and as a parent so far. We want you to consider some of the major aspects that are affecting your understanding and practice of parenthood. What are those stories that you are telling yourself about your kids' behaviours and the reasons behind the way you answer them? This is important because toddlerhood is increasingly recognised as a delicate stage where parents can really instil the basics for strong, resilient, and confident children. It is during such critical time that you want to work on your communication style and empathy to lay down the foundations for a healthy life long relationship with your children based on common values, cooperation, boundaries and respect for each other. So, how do we build a solid life-long relationship with our children based on nurturing common values and virtues? In this book you will find plenty of ideas and practices that will inspire and support you in your parenting journey. It is never too late to start and if you are here you are looking for inspirational ideas to implement in your daily life. Yet, before you can implement new ideas it is useful to stop and understand your own parenting approach and the generational patterns that are most natural to you. Self-understanding your mental models can help you recognise the triggers of your children's behaviours, take control of the way your deal with the interactions with your kids and find other ways if those ones are inefficient or waning. In this book you will find useful information on how to track and trace back your parenting model and how to move forward from it. This also includes the tools and strategies to implement effective tactics to discipline today's toddlers to let them thrive and reach their full potential despite all the digital temptations and distractions. We would like to introduce you to ways of keeping yourself mindful and positive with your children even when seriously sleep deprived, emotionally drained and juggling between the many demands of life. Keep yourself sane by finding time to look after yourself whatever that means by revealing the self-help tools that you can apply daily. At the Mindful Parent Academy, we have your and your family's well-being at our heart. You must try every possible way to keep yourself peaceful, happy, connected, and sane while the demands on you as carer and provider are never ending and your energy and patience are fluctuating. Enjoy your reading.

Introduction

The struggle is real: disciplining toddlers is so damn hard. They are so innocent in their mischievousness that they make it ever so difficult to enforce any rule. Toddlers are so adorable that they could get away with all sorts of misdeeds and they will still be loved and cherished. They can still make you smile while they turn you, and everything else around you, into a wreck. Toddlers are blissful creatures that come with no instructions but with plenty of vivacity, expectations and demands. And so, it should be. They are literally life in its full potential.

Parenting a toddler, or more than one simultaneously, can be exhilarating and astonishing at times. No matter how much you have been wishing and preparing to become a parent, by the time your bundle of joy has turned into a toddler at about 12 months of age, you have been developing several unimaginable super powers that you were totally unaware of. Just to name a few: you have never been so sleep-deprived and still functioning so well. You have never felt this exhausted but you still carrying on doing your duties and with added efficiency. You can be so attentive on following what s/he is doing that you can even see what s/he is doing from the back of your head. You have been anticipated many life-threatening incidents and saved his/ her lives on countless occasions. You have never felt so desperate for some peace and calmness that you have found a robotic silence inside yourself. No point stopping the chaos outside anyway. Toddlers can make you realize how much you can be strained and stretched and still bounce back with more profound love and fond enthusiasm. Toddlers are wonder-full and magnificent. They can gift you with glimpses of childhood and even heal the wounds of your inner child if you let them. So why we should discipline them and what is so difficult about it? What are the major struggles that most modern parents encounter?

At the Mindful Parent Academy, we believe that many new parents tend to have quite a 'romanticized' idea about raising a child and little information about what it is actually coming their way. Then again, as an old saying states: 'it takes a village to raise a child.' Well, where has everybody gone? In today's modern world, more often than not, people tend to live away from immediate family members and old friends. Not everybody is surrounded by supportive communities with free baby groups or parks and play centers.

You will definitely agree that raising children, particularly a toddler (or more than one simultaneously), can be, at times, a very draining physical, emotional and psychological experience. However, most of the time, it is still the greatest and most fulfilling experience of your life. Toddlers are amusing. They are pure fun. But only if they are in the right mood and in 'favorable' conditions. There are so many factors that could affect a toddler's mood and therefore the mood of the day and night: hunger obviously, tiredness of course, thirst, change of routine, overstimulation, under-stimulation, teething, 'terrible twos' (for some of them 'terrible threes'), losing a pacifier or a favorite toy, sleep regressions, growth spurts, being teased by a little friend, missed a nap, too long a nap, catching a cold, lack of some key nutrients, push for independency, separation anxiety, a major change in family composition, a new house, starting kindergarten and so on and so forth. The list of factors that can affect you toddler's mood can actually be endless. And only you, and other relevant carers, can try to figure out the source of distress.

Introduction

Any unmet need or desire of a toddler can trigger every parent's worst nightmare: A Tantrum. A tantrum is an uncontrolled outburst of anger and frustration. However, while a tantrum can last from under a minute up to ten minutes, a more serious incidence is a meltdown. This is a type of tantrum, in which emotions takes over the child and there is a total loss of control. While with a regular tantrum, a child can regain control of his/herself, a child having a meltdown needs someone to recognize their behavior, and needs someone to help them regain control of themselves. Both of these can happen to any child of any family. It should be expected. However, not all parents are equipped with the right knowledge and understanding to tackle these moments and, while in it, actually reinforcing that lovingly and reassuring relationship that every child is so in need of. And this is what this book is about.

All of this is to say that all children will be naughty at some point and even lose control of themselves sometimes. And this is a fact, so let's face it and accept it. It does not define you as parent, it does not mean you are not good enough, that you are a failure for not having children 100% happy at all times. Or for not being able to anticipate a trigger for her misbehavior. Particularly during toddlerhood, you need to stay strong because while you are extremely proud of your kid/s growing up strongly and happily, their brain is still developing and they can get trapped into very big emotions. However, what you want to avoid is to try disciplining your child during a tantrum, or worse, during a meltdown. Simply you are going to fail. Your child will simply be unavailable, unreceptive. You must allow their big emotions to flow out and to be released. To let them go. This though, does not mean you should accept bad behavior. You can allow all emotions within warm boundaries, but not all behaviors. This is because those behaviors can be dangerous for your child and others around them. This book is here to help you gain that knowledge and understand these delicate skills: to anticipate any potential trigger for misbehavior and give you the tools to help them navigate and master those big emotions. We believe that it is possible to meet our young children right there when they are at their worse and be at our best. We can intervene while they are losing themselves and help them ride their emotional roller-coaster back to their calm self.

On the other hand, to discipline a toddler is an all-embracing and ongoing practice that comes before any tantrum occurs. In this book, you will be first guided to reflect on some aspects of your parenthood approach that you have probably overlooked. You will gain a much clearer picture of your most important values useful to guide your daily practices with your children and your family life. You will be invited to take some actions in your daily life that will make you become that parent you aspire to be at all the time. You will learn the tricks to apply effective discipline strategies to tame those tantrums but also to establish respect for your family's core values in a peaceful and mindful way. Your child needs to trust you, to feel loved and appreciated by you, to express their emotions, and learn how to master these big emotions and misbehaviors. However, s/he also needs to know who is in charge and or what consequences follow a dangerous behavior, for instance, crossing the road on their own, handling sharp objects in the kitchen, biting and pushing others and so on. This book will enforce the idea that Balance is the key. Do not intervene all the time. Choose your battles. Be an observer, but make sure your child trusts your judgment about safety for his/her self and others. So how do you reach that so sought-after balance in a mindfully positive way?

What do you need to know to raise respectful and responsible little people based on your knowledge, experience, location and in the face of adversities?

Introduction

What is the basis for a long-lasting relationship with your children grounded on respect and mutual understanding? What are the core ideas of effective but toddler appropriate discipline?

This book will look at cornerstone topics such as:

- Mindfulness Tactics for Parental Stress Management, **Error! Bookmark not defined.**

- Communication style,

- Respect of values,

- Trust and Love,

- Sibling rivalry,

- Tools for more cooperative toddlers   **Error! Bookmark not defined.,**

- Listening to each other.

What this book mostly suggests is that if you can adopt a mindful approach in yourself in order to foster a positive parenting discipline, you will most likely set the basis for a healthy life long relationship with your child and your partner. And ideally, a mindful child later on in his/her life. But how do we achieve and maintain these long-term goals?

The book will explain the importance of being mindful as a precondition for a positive parenting approach. What does it actually mean to be (or aspire to be) a Positive and Mindful parent in the current world and how it can be linked to a guilt-free approach?

Introduction

The book will point at ways to try and reach a No Drama No Yelling home by establishing clear and solid boundaries while creating an emotional connection and warmth within them. It also suggests to have a completely alternative approach toward toys, playroom, play dates, sports, activities, and so on to avoid overwhelming your child and trigger misbehaviors.

The book will explore ways to communicate and connect with your toddler/s, the tools to redirect their actions, the tricks to recognize the triggers of a tantrum and avoid them, but also how to teach your children how to be responsible, respectful and cooperative. The main aim of this work is to equip all parents with the tools to manage their parenthood journey, knowing what to expect so that they can handle most situations in a calm and constructive way, avoiding yelling, establishing respect, managing tantrums while remaining deeply connected with their children and build that 'wonder-full' lifelong relationship that you will be so proud of. Let's begin!

Chapter 1: A New Born Mother and Father

When a baby is born, so is a mother and a father. Even if you have already had your first child, you are born as a parent of two, three, and so on. It is always different. It will always be a different chapter of your lives with new challenges and adjustments to be made.

Parenthood in modern times is stressful. The demands on parents are too high and too many. Often new parents tend to have a quite 'romanticized' idea of pregnancy, birth, and parenthood. And find themselves struggling when confronted with the reality of raising egocentric little people.

As a parent, you may find it especially daunting to be present, intentional, and attentive. You're pulled in dozens of different directions by the many demands on your time and energy. And your children instinctively know how to push every reactive button you possess.

They can sniff out when your emotional bandwidth is low and choose that moment to present their less-than-adorable selves. It's no wonder you see red-faced parents losing it when their children have public meltdowns or getting rankled when their preschoolers sulk at the dinner table.

It's hard not to react (or overreact) to your child's shenanigans, especially when you're stressed and overwhelmed. But even at your best, you'll find it challenging to know what to do and how to respond in irritating, emotionally charged, or embarrassing situations with your kids.

Before we carry on our journey though, we would like you to stop for a moment and take some notes, even just mentally if you can't write at the moment. Whatever you are doing stop for a moment and: Deep deep breath IN and… breath Out.. Focus on you. It is important to start reflecting on some very important areas of your life that might have been completely overlooked by you but that maybe are unconsciously directing and affecting your parenthood experience so far.

Have you ever reflected on your parenting style? Who are the parenting examples that you might want to follow? Or that you definitely do not want to follow? Such as your siblings, best friend, cousins? Think about it for a moment. Now focus on you again. Who are the figures or the traits that you would aspire to develop as a parent? Who do You want to be as parent? What are you going to do today in order to be that parent? What are your core values and are they Universal or particularistic?

Now, focus on your experience as child. Were your parents highly critical? Punitive? Strict? Uncommunicative? Often unreasonable? Offensive? Overly permissive or intrusive? Have you been neglected or abused? Have there been any tragic events in your family life? Do any of the above resonate with you? And are they influencing in any way your parenthood approach? In terms of your values, the way your deal with your children's misbehaviors and so on? Although, we appreciate that all parents have tried their very best considering their historical period, upbringing, knowledge and livelihood, it is also true that certain parenting traits can even go from one generation to another unchecked and have an impact in the way we deal with our children. Have a think about it.

What is your experience of Parenthood so far? What are the aspects you are particularly proud of? And the ones you feel guilty or not so proud of?

What are your feelings about yourself? Your post-partum body or your partner's post-partum body (if applicable). Your life in terms of being a carer and a provider? Friendship and family relations, including the relationship with your partner at the moment?

Please reflect on all of the above aspects because these can really affect your mindset, and as a consequence your daily life and your attitude towards others including, and most importantly, your little children.

Parenting your children and building a secure and happy home life for them is the most important job you'll ever undertake. If you enter it —or continue it— without any forethought or preparation, you're allowing in-the-moment circumstances and emotions to determine how you want to respond and make decisions.

Creating this blueprint is a mindfulness activity that ensures you have plans and tools available when you need them in high-stress moments. It also helps you shape your decisions about how you create boundaries for your children, how you choose to nurture and guide them, and how you spend your time as a family.

One of the best ways to discern your parenting values and guiding principles is through self-questioning.

Your answers to the questions we provide here will help you determine the actions you intend to take, both preemptively and in real-time, to support your mindful parenting commitment.

After you answer these questions and define actions, your next step will be to review the values and actions on a weekly or bi-monthly basis to ensure you're staying on track and making any necessary course corrections.

Your family and parenting values may shift over time as your children grow, and your lives change, so revisit them yearly to ensure they are still relevant and aligned with your principles for your family.

We suggest you and your spouse review the following questions and write your answers in a journal. Share your answers with each other and devise one value statement that reflects both answers or a compromise you decide on together. Then brainstorm specific actions you will take to support your value statements.

For example, for question one, "What is the general atmosphere you want in your home?" your value statement might be:

We want our home to be a place of calm and peace in which we prioritize quality time together, encourage healthy self-expression, and spend time talking, sharing, enjoying fun activities, and giving ourselves the time and space to recharge and find emotional balance.

Types of Parents

Researchers have stated that there are four types of parents: Authoritative, Permissive, Authoritarian, and Uninvolved. Authoritative is being perceived as the most reasonable and balanced of all other types, as they either have one problem or the other. In the cases of authoritarian and permissive, these two types are the extremes; the permissive is extremely lenient while the authoritarian is extremely controlling. However, the worst and most damaging type is the uninvolved. I will give a short explanation on each and how they can be exercised below.

The authoritative parent. This is the best method or type of parenting, the reason being that parents with this method are not overly harsh; neither are they extremely lenient. This is a mix of rules and freedom in which the kids are not subjected to only the will of the parents and at the same time know that there is a limit to how free they are. In this method, there are consequences for every wrong action, and there are rewards for, not all, but some positivity, your kid doesn't get a reward for eating, but you can sometimes reward your kid for some kind of display of obedience or any other thing you deem fit to be called a good deed, at least for a toddler, so as to make them keep the good deed up.

Authoritative parents:

- Let their kids know what they expect from them, morally, academically.

- Set rules and regulations that have consequences if dishonored; well-planned daily schedule for important and basic things that have to be followed duly, although not when extremely uncomfortable, and backed with reasons and explanations.

- Create a chance for good and regular communication, which promotes a strong parent-child relationship.

- Are not afraid to implement consequences for kids' wrongdoings.

- Make sure to keep promises made to kids.

This kind of parenting is the one that helps build kids' personalities; this mostly bears the fruit of self-confidence, self-belief, and high self-esteem.

The permissive parent. These are parents that allow "too much freedom" for their kids; they literally spoil their kids with a lot of consequence-free actions with the fear of not wanting to upset or offend their kids. This set of parents act more like "best friends" than parents. In permissive parenting, while showing a lot of love and affection towards kids, they tend to be overly lenient and delicate with them.

Permissive parents:

- Show so much love and affection towards kids.

- Give the mammoth rewards for kids' minutest efforts.

- Always try to avoid kids' anger, even if it requires not correcting them.

- Unlike the authoritative, have no rule or consequences and always willing to compromise even if there is any, so as not to tamper with their temper.

This type of parenting, however, doesn't help in the building of the child's personality as it most times result in a lot of negatives like self-centeredness, very low socialization skills which make it hard for them to build and keep good relationships with people, kids brought up with this kind of method tend to become very saucy, and have no regard for authority.

The authoritarian parent. A type of parent with very high conditions and code of conduct, the authoritarian is similar to the authoritative, in the sense that they both set rules and principles, but the difference is that the rules and regulations of the authoritative are detailed, but the authoritarian's are always overly strict and without any reasons or explanations. The authoritarian parents believe that children have no rights whatsoever to question their authority, once they say "go," it is "go," there is no "go because," "go so that," whatever they say is final!

Authoritarian parents:

- Do not believe kids have a say; they believe kids aren't to be heard, only to be seen.

- Give no reason for rules; they believe they have no reason to explain to their kids why rules and regulations are being set.

- Have no problem with using punishment as a means of discipline.

- Give their children little or no chance to make their own decisions or choices.

- Makes sure rules are obeyed no matter what.

- Don't give much time to a showing of affections and emotions.

The authoritarian type of parenting has a really strong effect on the confidence and self-esteem of the kid. The fact that they are never given a chance to affect their self-assurance. Parents that find themselves in this category might want to try and be a little softer for the child's sake.

The neglectful or uninvolved parent. This is a very harmful type of parenting in where the parent has little or no involvement in the life of the kid. This actually is not very common as no responsible parent would want to neglect their children, but some parents actually think this method aids in making the children strong on their own. Causes of cases like this can include, having no clue on how to handle their children, not wanting to invade their child's privacy, having jobs that require a lot of their time, and other numerous reasons.

Uninvolved parents:

- Give little or no attention and spend less amount of time with their kids.

- Have not-very-close relationships with their kids.

- Less involvement in their kids' outside-home activities.

This type is another type that can also affect the self-esteem of kids. Parents that find themselves in this category should do something about it, and try to adjust; if not, you might want to contact an expert for professional advice.

Some parents might find themselves exhibiting traits of more than one method, just be sure to choose the type that fits your kids, although the most advisable is the authoritarian parenting method.

Talking To Toddlers

The ability to communicate with our toddlers in a way that they can understand is an asset that every parent should possess, although it might not be easy, it is possible through the help of some key information that I will be sharing with you shortly. You don't want to live the nightmare of having your toddlers getting your message wrong or misinterpreted. There are ways by which you can be sure to establish a good communication with your kids, either when you're just talking to them or when the talk is for some discipline and correction. First, we discuss the approach to employ when talking to your kids; then we move onto the part where you implement discipline.

Tips on Establishing Good Communication with Toddlers

- **Speak normally**: You might be tricked into thinking that talking to your toddlers like they do makes them understand you better, no, in fact, it might even upset them, why? Because it might seem like you're trying to mock them. The truth is, what you call "baby language" is the best result of their effort to speak as we (adults) do. They are always eager to be able to do the things they see us do, but, like every person trying to learn something new, there is a slow beginning. Now, let me ask you this, as a person trying to learn how to play tennis, will you be pleased if your trainer drops the egg(ball) to bounce before hitting it with a bat instead of serving normally? And say it's because he wants to come down your level and make it easy for you. That only reflects your incompetence, and does that not seem like mockery? You can only get better when you practice with people that are way better at it than you because that's how you discover and develop new skills and techniques, the same goes for the kids. Also, it's only hard for them to speak; it's not as hard for them to listen and hear. Although it is good to try to come to our babies' level for better understand, it can only be advised in some other aspects, not while talking.

Note: They can only learn from the original, not from the imitation of their own sub-standard version.

- **Keep it short and simple**: too many words will confuse your toddler, so, it is advised that you keep your information short and simple, for a quicker, easier understanding, but be careful not to misunderstand a toddler's "quicker" for an adult's. Excessive words can sound like gibberish to toddlers, Imagine, extracting a question from engineering, mathematics to a second grader to do.

How to Talk to Toddlers When Trying to Discipline Them

- **Talk with subtlety**: Nobody, not even toddlers, want to be ordered around, so refrain from using a commanding voice. The mind is built in a way that it tends to defend itself against an imposing or enforcing authority; this makes the kid tend to refuse instructions that sound like orders. For example, instead of shouting, "Daniel! Stop bouncing on the couch," you could use, "Danny boy, mummy wants you to sit still on the couch" a little slow, that gives a tone of subtlety. Don't ever yell!

- **Find substitutes for NO!** Why do companies change their commercials from time to time? We get tired of what we are used to. When you always say no to your kids, they get used to it, thereby reducing the effect it has on them. Instead, try and erase that sense of negativity and replace it with some sense of positivity. For example, when trying to stop finger sucking, offer suckers, and say to them, "why don't you suck this instead, we don't want our fingers to get wet and smelly."

- **Avoid making threats**: It is natural in humans wanting to dare; we like to see what comes after a threat has been made. Therefore, refrain from adding "or else" in your instructions, it calls out the inbuilt daring nature, thereby raising the tendency of refusal to comply.

- **Show seriousness**: Like adults, toddlers like to get involved when they recognize a level of seriousness. Toddlers too can be severe at times, even though they can be very playful with almost everything. For example, you want Diana to stop hitting the perfume bottle on the shelf; you don't just sit where you are and ask her to stop, rather, you get up, go closer and make your point known, the fact that you got up from where you were seated, shows a level of seriousness about that subject matter.

Chapter 1: A New Born Mother and Father

Chapter 2: Be True To Yourself

Taking Care of Yourself

Parenting, in itself, is a tough job. Parenting toddlers is super tough. While you struggle to handle that little bundle of energy, oftentimes, you forget about yourself. We are so invested in the well-being and care of our little one that our own health and mental sanity take a back seat.

Toddlers are energy driven, curious beings. With their curious nature and ever-developing emotional repertoire, they unwittingly throw many challenges before us. Understandably, such challenging behaviors can strain our patience to breaking point and frustrate us to no end. It becomes, therefore, even more, important that you take a breather every now and then so you do not lose your own balance and control of emotions. Remember that if you lose control of your emotions and get exceptionally angry over your child, not because they have done something so unpardonable, but because you are so frustrated with the continued stress of misbehavior that a point comes where your patience breaks, you will only harm your child more. As innocent as toddlers are, they are incapable of doing something unpardonable that would deserve or justify the use of force on your part. It is important, therefore, to act before the situation reaches that boiling point, that threshold where things could tip over for worse.

Controlled Reactions

The best step that you can take as a parent is to take care of your own emotions in a timely manner. If you are working hard and struggling to teach your child emotional control and addressing challenging behaviors, it all comes to nothing if you yourself end up losing control of your emotions.

Many times, we as parents are tempted to simply shout, slap, or yell at our children. But, if you wish to be a positive parent, take care that your actions or reactions to your child are hasty and rushed. Make it a point to breathe deeply (remember the breathing exercises!) and calm yourself before addressing your child. Count at least up to ten to give yourself time to calm your mind and swallow that frustration and anger. This is an important step to practice before you talk to your child after a difficult situation or as a reaction to their misbehavior. Imagine what you could do to your child if you did not calm yourself and take the time to think clearly and with positivity before approaching them. Keeping this thought, and this realization always at the forefront of your being as a parent will help you reign in your emotions and not act rashly.

Self-Care

Beyond providing consistent and controlled reactions each time to every misbehavior, it is important to make your own self-care a priority. Allot time for taking care of yourself each day. But what exactly is self-care? It is like filling up your tank before you begin each day fresh and rejuvenated. It is giving your mind and body the rest it deserves. It is to give yourself the ability to handle your own social and emotional needs as an individual and not just as a parent. Self-care might is the last thing on your mind now when all your focus is on your toddler and giving them your best. But, you can't really give them your best when you are not your hundred percent self. Think of the safety instructions on flights. They always say that if the pressure in the cabin drops, you must put on your oxygen mask first before assisting your child. Of course, our initial instinct is first to take care of our child. But, if we do not get oxygen, we may pass out and will not be able to take care of our child or ourselves. The same goes for life. We must have our needs met so that we can care for our family properly. There are a few things that you can do to give yourself proper care. Plan to experiment with the different self-care strategies so you are able to decide what strategies work best for you.

Meditation

A short and quick meditation spell can help you feel refreshed. If you are new to the world of meditation, there are several resources available to guide you through various meditation techniques. Make a habit of meditating for at least five minutes every day, either in the morning or in the evening, so that you remain calm and rejuvenated every day. You can even include your child in your daily meditational episodes so that you both can benefit greatly from this important life skill.

Spending Time Outdoors

An excellent idea is to spend sufficient time outdoors near nature. It has been observed that simply watching the greenery for a certain period of time has a very soothing effect on the mind. Therefore, if you could squeeze time out to spend at least a little time per week at a place full of greenery, close to nature and its elements, it would be greatly calming and rejuvenating for you. Look for hillsides, riverbanks, mountain treks, waterfall resorts, or any such spots that you can easily reach for a quick refreshing trip. If once in a week is not workable for you, you could opt for other self-care techniques and keep outdoors to a minimum of once in a month or two.

Music

This is one of the easiest ways to stay calm and poised. Simply listen to any music that you like, which you are confident would calm you. You could listen to music at almost any time. Whether you are feeling stressed or not, you can simply tune into your favorite music as you go about your daily chores around the house. An advantage of using music to stay calm is there is no real need to set aside time to listen to soothing music. It can be done while you are busy with other work too.

Physical Exercise

Keeping physically active apart from all the work you do around the house will greatly help you stay fit and refreshed. A time and activity assigned explicitly for the purpose of the exercise will work positively on your mindset. If you are unable to hit the gym for some reason, simply taking a walk outdoors for at least fifteen minutes will do wonders for your positive approach to daily issues.

Maintain a Journal

If you are able to write your thoughts and feelings regularly in a diary or a journal, it would be greatly beneficial in relaxing you and emptying your mind of stressful thoughts and problematic issues. This can be a great tool to keep you positive and feeling good about your life. When things become tough, you can make it a point to just write down at least three things you are happy about and grateful for. This can become your own gratitude journaling exercise. It will help you retain a positive outlook on life and avoid feelings of excessive frustrations and annoyance.

Pamper Yourself

You could take time out to treat yourself with a few simple pleasures. These need not necessarily be luxuries. Simple things like an aromatic massage, a hot bath, some soothing music, lighting scented candles around the house, or drinking rejuvenating herbal teas can all be great ways to pamper yourself and give yourself some much-needed attention.

Spend Time with Family and Friends

If you can make time to get away from the busy schedules and the hustle and bustle of daily life to spend time with your friends, it would be a great way to unwind. Get some away time from kids by having someone watch over them while you take a much-needed breather. This will help you relax, and you will be able to get back in the groove after the retreat with more vigor and energy.

Get Away From Gadgets

Though it is usually assumed that watching something on your mobile or the television will help you relax, and it is valid to some extent, often times it is the contrary that is true. From one social app to another, you can simply feel stressed into replying to messages, emails, and whatnot. Instead, if you can spare time for a digital detox, it will be extremely beneficial for you.

Chapter 2: Be True To Yourself

Chapter 3: You Matter

Children tend to suck up most of their parents' energies and time. However, You are not just a provider, a driver, a cooker, a carers. You matter. You have needs. Adult needs. And so is for your partner or any other adult helping raising your children. You need your space and time, and so does your partner. This is essential in order to be relaxed enough when reconnecting with your child.

You need to take care of your emotions with the aim of coaching your children's big emotions.

In case your parenting background has been particularly negative; for instance, you have survived narcissist parents or abuses, you need to re-parenting yourself and avoid bringing the past misdeeds into your relationship with your kids.

Attempting to raise children, especially those who tend to be disobedient or those who have been spoiled for many years, can be very difficult. It usually takes a lot of thought and self-control not to resort to the things we usually do, the parenting methods and statements that we grew up with, and the language that has been woven into us. For many parents, yelling, punishing, sarcasm, name-calling, and threats seem to be the only ways they can make themselves heard.

However, these aren't the only ways. Worse, they don't work. Child psychologists have repeatedly pointed out that punishment, yelling, and discipline tactics that aim to subjugate children are ineffective because instead of the child feeling bad for what she has done and thinking about how she can make things better, the child then becomes defensive and starts thinking about revenge. When we resort to the type of harmful ways of disciplining children that many of us grew up with, we actually deprive our children of the essential inner process of facing their own misbehavior.

How to Stop Feeling Anxious and Guilty About Your Parenting Skills

It is impossible to be the best parent, you are capable of being when you do not take time to set your mindset. Regardless of how patient you typically are or how well you can manage stress, every parent has a breaking point. This breaking point is a stressful moment, where you are overwhelmed with your little one's behavior and at a loss for what to do makes it any better. Of course, that breaking point may come easier when you have added stress from work, finances, or home life, as well as when you are hungry or tired. You see, the key to being the best parent you can be sure you are in the right mindset first. This involves taking care of yourself and being sure you have the alone time you need to recharge when it's needed.

You Cannot Pour From an Empty Cup

It is not uncommon for new parents to feel they must dedicate every waking moment to their child. They are constantly interacting with their little ones during their waking hours and desperately trying to catch up on housework when they are asleep. While there is nothing wrong with being dedicated to your baby and home life, you cannot pour from an empty cup. Even parents who are at work during the day need time to 'refill their cup,' meaning they need to take care of themselves before they have the energy stores to care for others.

Finding time for yourself is about more than hygiene or relaxation. It is about finding time to nurture your relationship with your significant other, getting away for relaxation with friends, and getting time away from their toddler. Whereas babies require constant supervision, toddlers can play in safe environments with less supervision. Allowing them to play on their own also encourages their individualism and independence. These are things that allow them to explore and develop their personality traits. Allowing them to play on their own also allows you to observe your little one and the way they interact with their environment.

Strengthening the Bond Between Mom and Dad

Though not all toddlers grow up in a two-parent home, those that do should see mom and dad as a unified front. A major part of staying on the same page is finding time to nurture your relationship. You should feel comfortable talking to your partner about the blessings and pitfalls of parenting. They should support you in finding time for yourself to recharge. They should also be willing to spend time with your toddler, helping them learn more about the world around them, and sharing in the parenting experience.

The key to finding any type of coherence between mom and dad is having a strong relationship that you can build cooperation on. Make time for each other—not just to talk about your child, but to talk to each other and become closer. Get in the habit of relying on your partner. Be clear about your own needs and how they can help. Getting time away from your little one is also crucial for effective parenting. Parents in loving relationships need time to celebrate and grow their love to maintain a strong, supportive bond. Make the time for your partner. Of course, your toddler is more demanding and has greater needs. After all, they rely on you to cook for them, help them clean up, provide them guidance, and much more. Be sure your partner is not being pushed away in the meantime. You'd be surprised how much having a date night twice a month and spending a little bit of time without your toddler each night (even if it's cuddling and watching television) can help you bond with your partner and maintain the closeness in your relationship.

Get Enough Sleep

People often imagine new parents as those with dark circles under their eyes, unkempt hair, and stains on their t-shirt, walking like zombies in a sleep-deprived stupor. It can be difficult to be sure you are getting enough sleep, especially when your little one is not sleeping through the night yet. Fortunately, the toddler years come with an increased likelihood that your little one will not wake up for a middle-of-the-night feeding. You'll be able to get a few more hours of uninterrupted sleep than you did when they were an infant.

If you don't get enough sleep at night, find time to nap with your toddler during the day. Many new parents say this is easier said than done, as there is always something to do. Once the baby is down for a nap, it is easy to find yourself binging your favorite television show or trying to catch up on housework. Keep in mind that the television show and the messy house will still be there when you wake up. Try to at least rest your body while your little one is napping. Ideally, try to fit in some meditation or mind relations. Find some relating tracks that you love listening to and enjoy the feeling of mindfulness when your little one wakes up again. If you cannot afford a cleaner, try to do little and often. This might help you feel that you are at it, and the house is tidy (for your sanity). This also might prevent you from ending up having hours of house chores to carry out while having a toddler (or more) around. Another idea could be to stick a list of house chores to do in your kitchen and ask your partners, and/or other carers, to help tick them off the list while the day goes along. Another valuable option to consider is to see house chores as an activity to perform With your toddler(s). Toddlers love to be given jobs. We are obviously not suggesting child labor but! A simple house chores that they can be completely absorbed with while you are praising them for being helpful, can buy you that 15 mins to clean a toilet, peel those vegetables or sort the laundry. Think strategically!

Do the Things That Make Life Simpler

Some parents feel bad about taking the 'easy road' for their toddlers. However, what they don't realize is that there are things that you can do that are easier without compromising your child's care. Additionally, doing things a simpler way gives you more time. This means you have more time for doing crafts and interacting with your little one. You also have more time to yourself—which is critical to maintaining your sanity. Here are a few strategies used by those parents whom we would classify as 'experts.' They'll free up your time without sacrificing how effectively you are raising your toddler.

Take Advantage of Low-Maintenance Cooking

Crock Pots can be a lifesaver for parents, especially when they have errands, cleaning, or work to worry about during the day. Instead of stressing about dinner, you can throw meat, veggies, sauces, and whatever else you would like into the crock pot and let it cook on low. You don't have to worry about constantly stirring it or overcooking the meat, as this method of cooking lets many flavors meld together. There are tons of recipes available online if you don't know where to get started!

Find Things to Do That Include Your Toddler

There is nothing wrong with working out with your toddler in the room or putting them in a stroller and taking them for a jog. Another great tool plays dates. The other child will help your little one to socialize and give them something to do while you catch up with the other child's parent. This allows you to have a good time while encouraging your child's social development.

Join a Gym with a Playroom

Once your child is old enough, it can be useful to join a fitness center that has a playroom or sign up for classes designed for mums to bring their children with them, such as running buggies, mummy fit, and so on. Of course, you should always ensure the safety of the environment and the credentials of the play area supervisor before leaving your little one in their care. There are two major benefits to these types of centers. First, you get some alone time with your little one close by—but out of the way. Second, your toddler has the chance to interact and socialize with other kids in their age group.

Familiarize Your Toddler with Friends and Relatives

Children look to their parents for everything. They share a special bond from the moment they are born and all through their life. Even so, your toddler must have the chance to interact with family members and friends. These people form your support system. They are the people that you can trust your toddler with when you want to spend alone time with your significant other—or even if you just need a break. Starting these bonds early is important to preventing toddler freak-outs when mom or dad leaves the house.

Keep Your Little One Busy

A busy toddler is a well-behaved toddler (for the most part). When kids are busy, they are learning. Additionally, activities keep your toddler from falling into the trap of electronics like televisions, iPads, and other devices. You'll learn more about great activities for your toddler and family, as well as how to set limits and rules about screen time.

Set Boundaries

Your toddler is constantly picking up on new words that describe the world around him or her. While it is exciting as your little one learns new words, especially at first, it can be frustrating when they are rambling on, and you are trying to have a little quiet time. Keep in mind that your child is just now learning about all that goes on around them. They are going to have questions and want reassurance about the things they believe in the world. Their conversation is also an incredible learning experience, as they look to you for guidance on what is going on in their world.

Even though, you should help your little one as they explore, you should also get in the habit of setting boundaries for your toddler. This is especially true for stay-at-home parents and the child's primary caretaker. Let them know when you need a little time for yourself. Encourage them to play and explore on their own.

Eat a Well-Rounded Diet

On top of lacking sleep, many new parents do not eat the nutrition they need. It is so much easier to grab a handful of chips or a quick sandwich or microwavable meal, rather than preparing something healthy and nutritious. Besides, who has time to eat with all the demands that parenting has?

If you pay close attention that you binge on chips for lunch or make other unhealthy choices, you'll notice that the food you are eating is not nourishing your body. It may make you feel overfull, bloated, or sluggish. You may feel unfocused or tired. This is no way to be in the best possible state of body and mind for parenting.

Additionally, countless studies have proven that eating a healthy diet is essential for proper functioning and brain health. The foods that we eat provide the nutrition we need to thrive. Without it, parents might become agitated easier, which hinders their ability to think clearly and rationally when dealing with a cranky toddler.

Chapter 4: How to Be A Positive And Mindful Parent And Reach A Guilt-Free Discipline

Are you following a gentle parenting approach? A conscious parenting approach? Or do you not have a clue about it?

There is so much out there today that is even confusing if we are talking about the same thing or there are differences between all the possible options. This book suggests applying a Positive Parenting approach for disciplining your children. Let's look a bit closer:

Positive Discipline

1. **It is both firm and kind.** It promotes mutual encouragement and respect that strengthens the parent-child relationship during the teaching process. Children learn good habits by imitating their parents and other role models around them. Teaching, by example, is the best way to instill discipline.

   Be respectful and kind, even if you are upset.

   Refrain from yelling, humiliating, or calling him names to prevent him from copying you when he becomes upset over something in the future. Seeing you calm and composed while dealing with the situation teaches him that this strategy is better compared to panicking or getting mad.

Aside from that, kindness encourages your child to become more receptive to reasoning, calm down, and cooperate. However, it is important to remember that kindness in this context is not synonymous with giving in or permissiveness. You are still teaching him self-discipline, kindly, and firmly. You say NO but in a tone that is not mean or harsh.

Furthermore, you expect him to follow the limits you set and enforce consequences when he acts otherwise. This method helps your child practice cognitive thinking, helping him master skills that he will need to make more complex decision-making in the future.

2. **It promotes a sense of belonging and significance**. Positive discipline promotes a sense of connection, eliminating deep-seated fear of being punished or grounded. It can be demonstrated by communicating your discipline plan or rules, then explaining the consequences that you will enforce if when he disobeys or misbehaves.

If you are introducing a new rule or discipline technique, discuss it to your child, so he will know how to adjust. It should not come out of the blue. In this way, you are showing him that you are working together during the learning process. It will make him feel significant and more compliant to conform to the new rule, limit, or consequence.

It works well with older children who already understand the science and reasoning behind the discipline. Kids below the age of three find it quite difficult to understand the consequences or make a sound judgment because the prefrontal cortex of the brain is not yet developed. For this age group, redirection strategies should be used. Parents should understand age-related behaviors and enforce appropriate discipline techniques.

3. **It teaches essential life and social skills**. Positive discipline is geared toward the development of skills, problem-solving, cooperation, respect, and concern for others. All these factors are important factors for the child's development and ability to contribute to the larger community, school, and home.

4. **It leads to the discovery of personal power**. This kind of discipline invites children to discover that they are capable of doing great things. They learn it when they obey and do positive deeds, or when they receive an appreciation, praise, acceptance, or a reward.

5. **Its effectiveness is long-term**. Positive discipline prepares your child to adulthood. What he is learning now will effectively help him thrive and survive in the future.

The Core of Positive Discipline

To fully comprehend the rationale of Positive Discipline, it is important to understand its context as an approach to instill child discipline. It originates from "discipline," the Latin word which means teaching and comes from another term "Discipulus" or pupil. It is about teaching and providing vital learning that the pupil can use in his lifetime. But over the years, discipline becomes synonymous with punishing and not teaching.

Chapter 4: How to Be A Positive And Mindful Parent And Reach A Guilt-Free Discipline

1. There is no such thing as bad kids, only bad behavior

At the core of Positive Discipline is the general statement that "there is no such thing as bad children, only bad behavior." It is important for parents to bear in mind that kids are naturally good, and they have episodes of acting up due to certain reasons that they cannot voice out, especially when they are young and do not know how to process their emotions.

There are two factors behind the challenging behavior of your child- the sense of not belonging (connection) and the sense of significance (contribution). When one or both of these basic needs are not satisfied, the children find a way to fulfill it, even if it requires negative action. Dr. Dreikurs aptly put it by stating that "A misbehaving child is a discouraged child."

Calling the child as "bad" for doing something negative is not healthy for his self-esteem. It usually starts when your kid continually misbehaves or throw tantrums, and you are exasperated. While trying to calm him, you slip and label him as a "bad boy" unintentionally. You can forgive yourself after that slip and quote the famous cliché that you are just human and commit mistakes, but if you keep repeating it every time he does something wrong, it will be engraved in his mind and damage his self-worth.

Positive Discipline aims to help parents learn to objectify the behavior and cut the "bad cycle." For example, instead of telling your child when he hits his younger sibling that "that's bad" or "you're such a bad boy," you may say "it is not okay to hit your brother when you are angry because he does not share his toy" and then let him understand the harm that might happen to his brother. When you objectify his behavior, you are teaching him the cause and effect. By directly addressing the "bad behavior" without using the term "bad," you are encouraging your child to make better choices and avoid hurting other people.

2. Show the child how to resolve the problem, instead of pointing out that what he did is wrong

Redirecting the behavior of your child requires more than saying, "Don't do that" or "No." It needs skills to teach him right from wrong using calm actions and words. For instance, you catch your child before he can hit his little brother, instead of saying "No hitting" or "Don't hit," tell him to "Ask his brother nicely if he wants to borrow a toy." By giving him an alternative way to get the toy, you are showing him that asking is more effective than hitting.

If he already hit his brother, it is a must to be creative with your response. One good way is enforcing a non-punitive time-out, which technically is about removing the child from the stimulus that triggers his behavior and allows him to calm down. You can cuddle him when he is very upset, let him play in his room, or ask him to sit with you. After his emotion subsides, start explaining (not lecturing) why his behavior is inappropriate. Encourage your child to give other positive options that he believes will give him the result he wants, without hurting anyone.

To change his behavior, use discipline as a teaching tool. Rather than telling him not to hit his little brother, show him the correct and acceptable behavior that will resolve the conflict and prevent him from repeating the mistake.

3. Be kind, yet firm when enforcing discipline. Show respect and empathy

A child may insist that what he did was right, hence the importance of enforcing safety rules and consequences to prevent similar incidents in the future. Listen to his story as to why he did it and win half the battle by displaying empathy, but still impose the consequence of his action to make him learn from his mistakes. Empathy makes your child feel understood, lessening his resistance, and heightened emotions.

However, even when you are disciplining your child, be respectful, and when you overreact, apologize. It will teach him to respect you more and the people around him. You should behave the way you want your child to behave while showing your parental authority.

Look for the "why" behind this behavior, especially when you observe that there is a pattern. Sometimes, hitting a sibling is a silent message that he is jealous of the attention you are giving to the younger child. Whatever the cause, resolve the issue early to make your child feels secure and loved. Treat the root cause and not the symptoms.

4. Offer choices, whenever possible

Giving your child positive choices works like magic when disciplining him. An example is when you are trying to make him sleep, and he still wants to watch TV, instead of getting angry, provide choices. "Do you like to go to bed now or in ten minutes? Ten minutes? Okay, ten minutes and then off to bed."

This approach is a win-win solution because he gets to pick the option that is okay with him, and you are offering choices that are advantageous to you. For example, you are about to go to bed, but your child doesn't want to sleep yet, you can give him/her choices like: "You want to sleep now, or I will read you a bedtime story?" By not forcing him to do something and letting him choose, you prevent power struggle. You allow him to take charge and show autonomy within your parameters. To successfully use this technique, provide palatably, but limited choices. Eliminate options that are not acceptable to you and honor what he selects.

5. Use mistakes as learning opportunities for your child

Use every misbehaving episode as a chance to learn invaluable life lessons. Often, the child misbehaves to achieve what he wants or when he is bored. For instance, he throws and breaks toys when he does not like them anymore. Instead of scolding him, use the opportunity to teach him the idea of giving them to his friends or donating them. If he is bored, provide other interesting activities. This will teach him the concept of displacement or finding ways to be productive and prevent destroying his properties. By empowering him with alternatives, he will be adept at making wise choices, even if you are not with him.

Use mistakes to teach your child about right and wrong. He needs to know why he is wrong, or he will continue using the act to get what he wants from you or the people around him. Just be careful not to give long lectures that will make him feel bored. Use past examples of misbehavior to strengthen your points.

Chapter 4: How to Be A Positive And Mindful Parent And Reach A Guilt-Free Discipline

Chapter 5: The Science behind the 'Happy Mind'

What is Mind?

The research findings of how our brain rewards efforts which enhance the ability of our species to survive, surely, we're living in the happiest era in the history of mankind. After all, wild capitalism is parallel to wild nature in terms of brutality. In the modern world, we are constantly faced with the quest for survival. We set off to work early in the morning and return late in the day. In between times, we are constantly engaged in struggling to make ends meet.

The human brain emerged approximately 2.5 million years ago. Then, when few people were around to witness it, it tripled in mass, reaching the 1,500 grams of the modern human brain from that of Homo Habilis' 560 grams. All this progress took place during the so-called 'hunter-gatherer' phase except for the last 10 thousand years after mankind settled.

Therefore, within this period, survival challenges and their respective resolutions have shaped the human brain. As a result, we are trying to find our way through the modern world's super complexity using a control system designed for the primitive era.

Our out of date factory settings are the root cause of many of the problems we currently face—including unhappiness. However, unaware of this situation, we have become smug enough to believe that we have a perfect brain compared to other living creatures—a conviction that collapses like a failed soufflé under the lightest of scrutiny. Our fondness for sticking with our inbuilt conditioning makes us fall, time and again, in the same pit.

During my research, I came across a rich seam of data about lottery billionaires—clearly the popularity of the subject. I discovered a regular pattern in the lives of these billionaires. The moment they are in the money, they chase after the life they've always dreamt of naturally. In many cases, the unbecoming demands of relatives and friends forced them to leave their familiar surroundings, break with their past, and start a new life elsewhere. Surprise, surprise, they end up struggling to become a part of this new environment. Many are either defrauded or betrayed by their new friends and spouses.

Consequently, they exhaust their riches, ruin their social relations, and end up worse off than when they started. It's a bleak thought, I know, but regardless of their country or culture, young or old, educated or not, they followed a similar downward spiral to unhappiness, with some making the same mistakes over and over again. As in the case of the guy who hit the jackpot 3 times and still ended up polishing shoes.

The brain is fairly magnanimous in this regard and rewards our best efforts with a blast of another substance in its chemical arsenal: dopamine. We are relieved, grateful even. We feel good and happy. Therefore, while cortisol helps us withdraw from life's less enjoyable moment's dopamine gets right in there and points out what needs to be done for a better life, then sets us in motion.

If what we do is recognized and appreciated by others, our brain triggers a third hormone called serotonin, boosting our happiness once more. When we choose to work for the common good and contribute to the well-being of others rather than pander to our own self-interest, a fourth hormone named oxytocin kicks in. And takes us to an entirely different dimension. Confidence generated by oxytocin strengthens our resistance to challenge. In short, even though we are always rewarded for overcoming challenges on our own, the grand award comes if we function with the people around us and when our resolutions are accepted by them as well.

And of course, there is the dimension of physical endurance. In response to hard physical effort, the brain deploys another hormone: endorphin. This attenuates muscle pain, and endorphin allows us to continue our activities without performance loss. Although the primary function of endorphin is to mask physical pain, it also counters the effects of cortisol. That's why at times of stress, leaping about a gymnasium in our Lycra leggings helps us feel good.

What Caused a Happy Mind?

We descend to earth in the second square, babies totally dependent on others. To survive, we need someone to feed us, put us to sleep, take us to the doctor when we're sick. In short, we need to be completely taken care of. Taking care of these demands isn't easy for our parents, but thanks to oxytocin, they take great pleasure in taking care of us. Besides, oxytocin enhances a solidification of mutual trust and affection; it makes us a family. Many people marry and have children so as to amass enough joy that oxytocin can provide them with.

Our struggle for independence starts the moment we are born. Our desire is to escape the Second Square and move into the Third. At first, achievements such as learning to speak, crawl, and walk fill us with hope. Everything we do is applauded by our family, and this triggers the release of serotonin, which evokes feelings of superiority.

We begin to think that we have the power to dominate and get everything we want. The bubble bursts when other kids get involved. The happy chemicals supplied unconditionally by our parents in our inner world cannot be found in the outer world. Even though we can't name them, we discover that dopamine comes from success; serotonin from appreciation and oxytocin from establishing strong friendships. That's how our battle to move to the fourth square kicks off. Showing others how important we are and proving ourselves becomes our priority. We strive to trigger these three chemicals. Some add endorphins to their happiness cocktail, with sport become an integral part of their life. These types can often be found running up mountains, white water kayaking. If over time, we establish relationships based on the trust we may manage to transfer ourselves to the fourth square. We can easily activate the happy chemicals because the contributions and support of others help us achieve success earlier. Besides, we will have people around us to appreciate our accomplishments, and their presence gives us a feeling of security in hard times.

Those who fail to gain such support over time may give up their efforts to establish meaningful relationships and end up back in the third square. Achieving success and feeling superior to others becomes their top priority and purpose in life. They are often surrounded by false friends (the worst kind). In successful times, they cannot find anyone to congratulate them with sincerity.

They accuse those around them of jealousy. Their bitter feelings prevent them from enjoying the pride and joy for their achievements. They hide their fragility and craving for love behind a mask. Some hide their true feelings with fake smiles to present a rosy picture to others. Yet, nothing they do can substitute for the serotonin and oxytocin gap; they can't find true happiness. In short, the people in this Square might be gloriously successful, but not as happy in the true sense.

What about those who fail to make any personal achievements—the people in the Third Square? They have two choices. Those who choose to obey go back to the Second Square. They win the love of people whom they see as their protector and leader by pampering them. Gaining the support of powerful people gives them a sense of security. However, failing to accomplish something on their own eats them up and leaves them with a feeling of lowliness. They may lead to a peaceful but unhappy life.

Chapter 6: How to Have Thriving Thoughts?

Gratitude

Practicing gratitude places the focus clearly on what you have as opposed to what you don't have. There are many reasons we are encouraged to do this. For starters, whatever you concentrate on increases in your life, just as whatever you focus on when you take a picture clearly defines the subject and quality of the photo. What you bring into focus in your life, you talk about, you think about, and you end up drawing to you. If you focus on poverty and bills and lack, you attract more of that. Most people don't realize that they continually communicate with God. You put out your energies, and he answers. The subconscious does not know imagination from reality; it only knows what you think about all the time and how you feel about it. So it figures, if you obsess about your crummy relationship with your spouse, you're terribly disobedient children or your ramshackle house, that must be what you want, and it takes you at your word and sends you more of it.

There's a little saying, "Count your troubles; you'll be sad; count your blessings; you'll be glad." It's relatively simple. Instead of always complaining about your disobedient kids, start being thankful for them, for the way they think, for the opportunity to raise them, and for their strong and varied personalities. Rather than worrying about how everything has gone wrong with your house, try to thank God for a roof over your head and concentrate on the charm, the affordable house payment, and the fun you have decorating. And even though your spouse may not be perfect, he or she does have great qualities, and there are surely things that you appreciate about being married. Start being thankful for those things and see how quickly your life seems to change.

The amount of happiness and joy you have in your life is directly related to your ability to acknowledge what you are grateful for. Studies have shown that among the leading characteristics of strong families is the ability to express appreciation: not only for what each does but for who they are.

I recently met with a husband who told me that his new wife changed his life because she expressed her thanks to him for everything, even the small things that we tend to overlook. It has made a huge difference in their marriage—as well as their outlook on life. Even when you are not in the presence of your spouse or kids, talk about them in a positive way. Convey to your friends and coworkers how grateful you feel for them. Your outlook and attitude determine the direction of your life—not the external things that seem annoying or wrong at the moment. You captain your own ship. You select the course of your life. You are not a victim in any way—unless you choose to put yourself in that role. A victor sees where he or she is going and enjoys the journey. Gratitude helps you get there. As a matter of fact, you can't get there without it. You will keep circling and circling, getting tossed around on the waves you focus on.

This is what happened to Peter in Matthew 14. The wind and waves were crashing all around, but Jesus walked on the water. When Peter wanted to walk on the water, Jesus told him to get out of the boat. For a moment, it seemed like he would be able to do it, but his focus changed from Jesus to the chaos and danger swirling around him, and he began to sink. That's when we begin to go under too. When we take our eyes off of the good and focus on what bothers us, we spin down a spiral of despair that sucks us under.

What you focus on increases. Don't wait, always looking toward the future for what you will be thankful for one day. Be thankful for what you have today. Make a practice of being grateful. Make a mental list before you get out of bed in the morning or before you drift off to sleep at night. Write a gratitude list when you feel overwhelmed and tempted to get anxious or depressed. What is working; what do you have? Focus on that. It's important to be thankful in all circumstances. Without our trials, we would not grow. Without those challenges with our children, we wouldn't recognize our own weakness. Our spouses and children serve as our best teachers. They show us where we are now and where we still need to go.

You may think that you are fine the way you are: that you don't need to grow. Yet consider the laws of nature. Anything that stops growing is dying. The same goes for you and your relationships. I know it's much more comfortable to just be the way you have always been and do things the way you've always done them, but are you really happy that way? From what I have seen as a therapist, I tend to agree with Henry David Thoreau when he said, "The mass of men leads lives of quiet desperation." Chances are: you are one of them. This need not be true! Start to see things in the encouraging and bright light of gratitude. It takes no time and no special skills, and you can start immediately.

Now you might say, "Yes, but you don't know my situation. My life is filled with troubles. I can't just turn into a 'Pollyanna' and expect them to disappear." All I can say in response to that is that it's up to you. You can stay where you are, but you don't have to. You can always find plenty to be thankful for. And not only will it benefit you to begin this practice, but it will benefit your kids even more because you will teach them to start this practice early in their lives, and their lives will be that much better because of it. So if you don't do it for you, do it for your kids.

Kids who are taught gratitude are less likely to have the "entitlement" mentality that we see so often today. When a child feels content, he or she experiences less stress and resentment, resulting in better overall health. As we all know too well, stress hormones released into the body that has no outlet for release impact your immune system, your heart, and other organs, and they decrease your resistance to disease.

Over the years, there are many suggested ways for clients to make gratitude, fun and memorable and to strengthen it into a habit. For example, give each of your kids a roll of toilet paper (or paper towels, shelf paper, or whatever you might have handy) and have them fill out each square with things they are thankful for. You can give a little prize to whoever thinks of the most.

A Note About Competition

Competition is not the enemy. It can be used to spur each other on to greatness. The important thing about competition is to promote good, healthy principles of sportsmanship. Competition can be harmful when used to pit one sibling against the other. "Why can't you be more like your sister?" "David gets good grades; what's wrong with you?" "Annie is definitely the prettier of the two girls." "Dustin is clearly the athlete; Josh seems to only like art. I don't know what to do with him." These statements clearly foster harmful competition, creating a space for kids to feel resentful toward a sibling because Mom obviously prefers one over the other.

Creating a fun atmosphere that nurtures good-natured competition can encourage a child to be the best he or she can be. Games to promote certain characteristics (such as gratitude) can help. Encourage kids to find nice things to say to each other—to express thanks even for the little things. Writing thank-you notes is another way to do this. Such a habit teaches kids not only to be focused on what they get but to express gratitude to the giver.

Thanking God for all your blessings is so much more pleasant than praying for him to make you well when you get sick; yet, unfortunately, that is what most of us do. We forget to acknowledge the good things in our lives, but when we get in trouble, we run to God and ask him to fix it. Perhaps if we practiced active gratitude for our health, our good appetites, our strong bones and muscles, our prosperity, our skills and talents, and our relationships, we might be less likely to get sick in the first place.

Studies have shown that people who practice gratitude regularly are less likely to show symptoms of depression and experience higher levels of life satisfaction than those who do not. Having higher levels of life satisfaction leads to a better quality of sleep, which is important in maintaining a healthy lifestyle. It is obvious that it feels more fulfilling and less stressful to be in a relationship with someone who appreciates you than one in which you feel taken for granted.

Since gratitude leads to greater contentment, you will be less likely to judge others. This leads us to our principle: limit judgments.

Chapter 7: Happy Parent Happy Children from the Start

Integration is the key: Between the parents and their child. It is about a balance between "no too much", "no too little" differentiation. Lack of differentiation: parents that don't go to the gym, don't work, don't have me-time, etc. Their life is only about the kids and this may because children might not develop fully and the effect is in all aspects of life from the 'bedroom' to classrooms etc. The opposite is too much differentiation.

How does the relationship with your kid/s shape the way your kid develop their mind and build relationships around them?

Consciousness and integration need to be joined.

Empathy overreaction. Go and meet them right there. Be present even if just for 10 mins a day. Always talk about your kids about how amazing they are, talk to your friends about your struggles only when the child is not present.

Boundaries and routines with a 12- to 18-month-old are very important. Routines are imperative to all child learning and a critical part of healthy development. This is because routines contribute to the child's sense of safety. They also invite repetition, which is critical to brain-building. Plus, behavioral routines like teeth-brushing and physical activity can even influence long-term health. Let's start with play and sleep—two of your 12-month-old's most valuable routines.

Maybe you are not paying attention to your young toddler's routines because you are very busy or "going with the flow." You might also have your child in daycare and simply not know much about their schedule during the day. That's okay. Skip to Noticing Your Toddler's Schedule in this section and begin there. Determining your child's schedule is as easy as making a record of their play, eat, and sleep times each day and then stepping back and noticing any patterns. Once you notice your child's typical metabolic patterns (when they are hungry) and sleep patterns, then you can begin to become more predictable and intentional about the routines discussed in the following sections. Predictability and intentionality are very important in creating the kinds of routines that facilitate your child's health and well-being.

Playtime

Playtime is one of your child's most treasured routines. At this age, your child needs a minimum of four 20-minute periods of dedicated play with a responsive, valued caregiver. It is very important that you set aside several moments to stop what you are doing and engage your child in attuned, responsive play. You should also be playfully engaged when you are simply in the room with them but busy doing other things. This exercise is an opportunity to expand on the skills that are most important during the dedicated playtime moments. We call this "floor time" because parents should be on the child's level.

Parental Authority

Authority is the foundation on which your discipline depends. Without respect for your authority, your child is not likely to give consent to what you want. His respect for your power can base on love, so your child goes along with what you want because he values you and your relationship. Or that respect can be found on fear, so that your child dreads knowing what will happen if he or she doesn't go along with what you want, because of the hurt you might inflict.

Parental Modeling and Example

You are the most important teacher your children will ever have. You set the Mold in terms of what it is to be an adult in this world, and they will copy you in many ways. You will see that, even as they are well into their adult years. Of course, you don't have to be perfect, but do the best you can in being an honorable human being, and discipline issues will somewhat fall into place.

Fear-based authority can be costly to your relationship. Children learn to use distance, distrust, and deception as strategies to keep the scary power at bay. If you want a close and trusting relationship with your children as they grow, do not resort to threat, force, or intimidation to get your disciplinary way. Instead, create a safe connection of sentimental value that your child can truly respect.

Why It's Important

Your child must give you consent—that is, agree to do what you say—for your authority to take hold. However, parents should not ask their child for permission to be granted this authority in the family. Parents must assume power if they expect it to give. They must act like they are entitled to it. They must work in charge. They must expect to be respected, asserting authority in a manner that encourages the child's respect—not by abusing the power of their position.

The influence of your authority is less dependent on your power to dole out positive or negative consequences than you might think. It's more a matter of conveying a firm and confident attitude: "I mean what I say, and I will do what I can to help you behave responsibly." This attitude communicates the firm belief that, among other responsibilities, your job is to establish and enforce rules for the safety and well-being of the child, and that those rules shall obey.

Fact

A family is not a democracy with elected leaders, where each family member has an equal vote. A family is a benevolent autocracy, where those with caretaking responsibility—the parents—are in charge of governing those who are dependent on their direction and support—the children.

A parent who wants to be his children's friend, or who feels insecure or uncomfortable assuming authority, is soon going to be exploited by children who come to understand how much power they have in the family. Unable to set practical limits and to make practical demands, this parent increasingly lives by the children's terms. Children now set the behavioral plan in the family by dictating wants or threatening upset if their desires deny. The parent tries to please, tiptoeing around unpopular issues, not wanting to upset the children, indulging them to avoid conflict, placating them to keep the peace. This is the worst-case scenario— when a parent is unable or unwilling to assume authority.

The Dangers of Not Having Authority

Why would parents not assume authority? Some people grew up with such stern or harsh parental authority that they go to the other extreme to avoid inflicting similar suffering on their child. "I don't want to do to you what my parents did for me." Some people fear to assert adult authority because it creates inequality with their child. "I don't want to be your boss if it gets in the way of being your friend."

Some parents crave their child's approval. "I can't stand your being displeased with me." Others lack the confidence to assume adult authority. "I don't know how to take tough stands and make them stick." Some parents never had a model of sufficient parental jurisdiction to follow. "My parents were Hands-off—they never made me do what I didn't want and never stopped me from doing what I did."

By not assuming meaningful authority, parents risk encouraging their child to gather more power to control himself and the family than is healthy. Parents risk eroding their effectiveness and self-respect as parents. They also risk shaping a self-centered child who may have problems accepting healthy limits in relationships and abiding by standard social rules.

Imagine that your child begged for a real live rabbit for Easter. Now a few weeks down the road, when you remind your child about caring for the rabbit, she attempts to place the responsibility back on you, as she's "too busy." Do not let this happen. Stand firm, even if it makes you momentarily unpopular. An agreement is an agreement, and this is part of your authority, to enforce the agreement.

Authority is part of the leadership that comes with the job of parenting—directing aspects of the child's life, enforcing adherence to those directions, and gradually turning over more power of authority as he grows older and learns to lead himself responsibly. This, of course, is the parents' ultimate objective: to put themselves out of the parenting business when the adult child is ready to assume responsibility for becoming the governing authority in his own life.

Establishing Parental Authority

If you feel uncomfortable asserting authority, can you learn to exercise this responsibility? Yes. You can practice several simple authority behaviors that all communications that you are in a position of authority. Simple acts of power include:

- Requesting information or asking questions about the child's life: "I want to know."

- Confronting issues in the child's life that you want to discuss: "We need to talk about this."

- Making demands for actions to be taken: "You need to do the following before you go."

- Setting limits on freedom: "You're not allowed."

- Expecting that agreements and promises are kept: "I will hold you to your word."

- Repeatedly insisting that an activity accomplished: "I will keep after you until you get it done."

- Applying consequences (both positive and negative): "You have to work off the damage that you did."

- Advising the child on the best course of action: "In my opinion, this is what you need to do."

- Controlling what kinds of support you will give and what kinds you won't: "We won't buy you those kinds of clothes."

- Making judgments about what is going right and wrong in the child's life: "In our judgment, you handled that situation very well."

By practicing behaviors such as these, with sincerity and without backing off, parents will establish their authority. Do not use threats to assert your power. A genuine threat inspires fear, while an empty threat is like a broken promise. It causes the child to lose trust in your word. Commitments work well than threats: "If you choose not to do what I asked, then I will do what I said." Fear and threats are to minimize, as this is not the true meaning of discipline and authority. You usually will not have to resort to punitive measures.

The Authority That is Positive

Authority is not just about correction. Another side of authority is contributive. As a parent, you exercise contributive authority by providing positives in your child's life that you control—resources, permissions, encouragement, help, support, advocacy, protection, knowledge, instruction, coaching, and praise, for example. Generally speaking, the more you have to correct, the more you should also demonstrate the positive, contributive side of your authority. Otherwise, your child will begin to feel that your influence is all negative when it is not.

Contributive authority is particularly important in second marriages where one partner is now stepparent to the other's child. Before the stepparent even thinks of exercising corrective authority, he or she should establish a base of contributive power with the stepchild. In the beginning, the biological parent should be the one providing any correction. The stepfather or stepmother needs time to build up a solid base of real authority before beginning to enforce corrective discipline. If the stepchild has been given no favorable jurisdiction on the part of the stepparent to accept, then he or she is unlikely to take the negative.

Chapter 8: Establish Respect

Respectful Parenting is Not Passive Parenting

Respect, although is commonly used, can be a controversial and unclear idea when you think about it or when trying to put it into practice.

First of all, Respect for what?

It can involve multiple values and principles. What are those? Are they Universal? Or are they particular to you or your family, community and/or nationality?

What are you going to teach your children that you have been taught (by your family or life experiences) and what you want your children to learn that you wished was introduced to you?

What are your values? And which one is important for raising respectful and responsible children? Some core values that many parents think are actually very important are: respect for others, kindness, diversity, gender, anti-racism, social justice and fairness, empathy, respect for the environment, clean eating, active lifestyle, mindfulness, and so on. Have you thought about your most important values and how to pass them on to your kids in an appropriate manner so that it feels natural to them to act in certain ways? For instance, let say you care about the environment, and you want to instill good manners and respectful behaviors in your toddler. It should follow that when unwrapping a snack, should be natural for your kids to handle you back the wrapping paper or to look for the bin. In order to teach that behavior, start at home by encouraging your kid to mimic you and invite them to use the bin every time they have a wrap to throw away. Let them familiarize themselves with the idea of recycling by drawing their attention to the rubbish tracks (that most of them love anyway). Ask them to help you with the recycling and bins in your house. When you are at the park or outside in general, comment on the beauty of trees, plants, and flowers and introduce them to the wonderful job they do for us. Trees provide us with the air that we breathe, shade for our picnics during the hot days, a shelter for little animals like birds' nest or squirrels. Flowers provide the pollen for our honey and so on. If and when your toddler pulls leaves from the bushes or plants or kicks a tree, intervene on their behaviors and explain that it is unfair and disrespectful. This is just an example of how you should proceed in order to establish respect in your little ones. Proceed in the same way for any other topic you feel is important to you, your family, and that is important to learn about in those early stages.

Patience and consistency are the keys.

Can little people get values? The answer is: the earlier, the better. However, you should aim to have a clear overarching frame agreed between you and your partner and relevant carers (or just with your-self if lone parent) about what are the core values and principles that your children must learn from early stages.

Remember, though, respecting children means respecting their stage of development, not reacting as if they were our peers.

Lead by example: if you snatch toys from your child to let him/her sit down for dinner, you should not be surprised if it does the same with other children.

Many parents stay at work all day and resent leaving their children at home with no activities to do. If television is not an option, this should be agreed with carers, and the greatest tip of the pedagogue is to create a daily agenda with the tasks that children must do after school.

Write down on a paper, the activity and time that the task should be completed. Vary activities each day. You have to be a bit methodical with the child. Leave a clear and objective list with bath time, television (if any), structured activities, and unstructured play time. Create a consistent routine, teach him how to organize room space. Organization is very important.

Another good tip is to set aside time for free activities. The little ones are going to adore this!

Are days when your little angel looks more like a little devil?

Here are some good practices for educating and disciplining your child, which have been gathered from across viewpoints, training, and curriculums:

Educating and disciplining children implies, among other things, establishing clear rules and limits. This is not always easy, even more so these days, but if parents adopt positive educational practices early on, it is possible to prevent future difficulties and problems. Cláudia Madeira Pereira, a clinical and health psychologist with a doctorate in clinical psychology, points out some good practices that will make this task easier:

1. Talk to Your Child

Even if you are exhausted after a day at work, take some time out of your day to talk to your child. At dinner or before going to bed, ask him how his day was, using phrases such as "Tell me what you did today," "Tell me about the good things that happened today," or "Did something bad happen?"

If your child is having a bad day, he can resort to several solutions. First, allow him to speak and listen to him without judgment or criticism. If you prefer, look for positive aspects that you can highlight and praise. Also, tell him about "what" and "how" to better deal with similar situations in the future.

2. Pay Attention to Good Behavior

Sometimes children learn that bad behavior is the best way to get parental attention... This is especially true for children whose parents pay attention to them only when they misbehave, even if that attention is negative, scolding them and rebuking them.

In order for your child to see that the best way to get their attention is through good behavior, praise him, her, and/or offer affectionate gestures (giving him kisses and hugs) whenever he does or even tries to do something good, such as helping set the table or doing a message, for example.

3. Promote Your Child's Autonomy and Responsibility

Some tasks, such as dressing in the morning, can be difficult for children. Even though it would be quicker for you to dress your child, you would prefer to encourage their autonomy and responsibility. Help your child by giving short and simple instructions on how to do the tasks.

To do this, use expressions such as "Take off your pajamas," "Now put on your shirt," or "Finally, put on your pants." Finish with a compliment, using phrases like "All right, you did a good job!" Sometimes it will not be enough to tell your child what to do; you may need to show him "what" and "how" to do it.

4. Establish Clear Rules

Be clear with your child about a set of rules. First, explain the rule succinctly and concretely. Second, make sure your child understands the rule and knows what is expected of him. In order for your child to be able to respect the rules more easily, try to give clear and simple directions, empathically and positively.

Phrases like "It's time to go to bed. Let's go to the room now, and then I'll read you a story," usually work. It is common for children to challenge the rules in the early days, but stay firm and consistent. Repeat as many times as necessary so that your child realizes that the new rule is to be followed.

5. Set Limits

When you need to correct your child's behavior, try to be patient, and stand firm. Tell your child that a certain behavior must stop, explain the reasons, and inform him of the consequences of not obeying. In that case, preferably use phrases like "If you keep doing, then..." Immediately and consistently implement the consequences whenever bad behavior occurs.

But do not resort to punishment or physical punishment (such as beating), as they only aggravate children's behavioral problems. Prefer to take a hobby or an object appreciated by your child for some time.

6. Stop the Tantrums

Although it is not easy, try to ignore the tantrums, not paying attention to the child at such times, as long as there is no danger to the child, of course! If possible, step back and pay attention to it only when the tantrums stop so that your child realizes that they can only get their attention when they stop throwing tantrums. At that point, prepare yourself, because your child will put him to the test.

At first, it is normal for tantrums to get worse. However, by systematically applying this method, the tantrums will eventually disappear. Remember that what you want with this is that your child learns that tantrums are no longer a good way to get what you want and that the best way to get the attention of parents is to behave well.

To achieve this, you must be aware of your child's good behavior and value these behaviors whenever they occur, for example, by giving a compliment, a kiss, or a hug. If you do, the child will feel more accompanied.

Open Communication is the Key

Communication is important in any relationship. It is also a good way to express love. Although it is good to exercise your authority as a parent when you communicate with your child, sometimes, you should lighten up a bit and just have fun and relax. Instead of talking about changing some undesirable behaviors, talk about pleasant stuff, and have a good laugh with your child. There are moments when the best way to solve a problem is simply by not giving it any attention by talking about other things that are positive in nature. By communicating with your child, he will not just feel loved, and you will also get to understand him better, and perhaps, you will also know the reasons behind his tantrums and other frustrations.

Listen

If there is one skill that all good communicators value the most, it is able to listen. Remember that communication is a two-way conversation. Therefore, do not just focus on doing all the talking. Instead, let your child talk and express himself. When he or she feels that you are listening, he or she will be more open, and it will also lessen his or her frustrations. Listening also means being open. Do not get mad at your toddler if the reason behind his or her misbehavior is not clear to you. Perhaps, he or she might start biting simply because he or she is teething. In such case, you cannot blame your child for biting.

Children act out mostly when we are frustrated, angry, stressed, and so on. Talk to your child about your feelings. E.g. 'mommy did not sleep a lot because of the baby, so mommy feels grumpy today' and so on…

Do not shame your child because of their tantrum, but comment on the situation 'you are very tired and this is why you are hitting and not sharing. Let's go home now.' And then go home NOW.

Always give hugs, kisses, and say, 'I love you.'

Raising psychologically, socially, physically, emotionally, and mentally healthy children are not about setting high expectations and strict rules. Instead, it is about showing children unconditional love, healthy communication, and reasonable expectations. It is about balance and providing the right environment that will nurture his total development.

Administration

The relationship between the parent and the child is central to the development of physical and mental health, cognitive and social-emotional functioning, as well as academic success. Aside from giving the basic needs, parents are also expected to chart a trajectory which promotes the toddlers' overall health and well-being. The child's experiences during toddlerhood impact the course of his life. His brain is developing rapidly during this period and assimilating what he sees, learns, hears, and experiences. He relies on his father and mother to survive and thrive. For a young child, his parents are the most important people in the world.

Parenting is regarded as the primary mechanism of socialization, which makes parents as focal persons to train kids, help them meet the demands of the environment, and teach them to take advantage of various opportunities. These vital tasks are continuing processes to help them survive and thrive.

The parents' main responsibility is to introduce children to the social world, helping them find their place and value in society and develop healthy self-worth by making the right choices. The way parents cope with the challenges of parenting enriches the lives of children, shaping the circumstances that help them build and refine their raw skills and knowledge.

One of the central aspects of development is attachment security, which influences the child's self-esteem and confidence that no matter what happens, his parents or caregivers will nurture his needs. The quality of attachment is dependent on how parents interact, communicate, and respond to these needs, especially during low moments. Consistency, appropriateness, and immediate response are also defining factors of good parenting. Children who are securely attached to parents have a more solid foundation that helps them establish strong relationships and empathize with others. Those with unsecured attachment have insecurity, disruptive social and emotional issues, and mental health disorders.

The Power of Empathy

Being an empathetic parent is the best gift a parent can give to their child. Your empathy for your child will let them understand that you actually 'get them.' Just like adults need someone to show confidence in them and acknowledge their feelings, so do young kids, especially toddlers. We need an understanding shoulder to lean on and cope with our time of distress. That shoulder will only be supported when the person understands where we are coming from and what the reason for our present situation is.

Toddlers are no different. They need us, parents, to be those understanding shoulders for them. We can become such strong support for them only by showing empathy. It is essential for kids that we understand them and their needs. For toddlers, their emotional needs and their feelings are of paramount importance. For us, a crying, whining, screaming, thrashing child might be just that, a child behaving undesirably. More so when according to us, they are doing so for no real reason and 'nothing.' But for them, it is hugely important. How many times have we encountered parents who defend their ignorance of their child's needs by saying it was 'nothing'? For us, it indeed might be nothing, but to them, it is as essential as the world.

Being empathetic toward your child gives you the space to see the world through their eyes. It makes space for your feelings without any judgment. Empathy is the great affirmation that toddlers need that tells them, "I understand how you are feeling. It's alright. Your feelings matter to me."

Empathy lets your child feel connected to you. It gives them a sense of belonging and security. They will be more at ease, knowing you are someone who understands them. It will bring more confidence in your relationship with your child. Children who have empathetic parents are more comfortable to "manage" and workaround. They live with the knowledge that they have support to fall back on bad days. If the parent is always critical and lacks empathy, the child will retreat within themselves. Such parents may be unable to foster a relationship based on trust and confidence with their kids. Such children will build resentment toward parents as time goes by. Empathy gives them the validation their feelings need.

The very first step to validate is welcoming of their mistakes. You are not accepting their behavior, instead of appreciating the fact that they are humans and will make mistakes just like you do. We taught from our early childhood that mistakes are bad, and the ones committing errors are wrong. We explained that making an error is akin to failure. What we need to realize is that children are innocent. They aren't bad; they are pure. But when we are not welcoming of their mistakes, we are saying the exact opposite to them. When you are accusatory in your approach, kids resort to hiding and covering up their mistakes because they fear you. Hiding mistakes can never be a good idea, as one lie would need a hundred more to hide it. This is not a good trait to encourage in your child. When you hide wrongdoing, you can neither rectify it, nor can you learn from it to avoid it in the future. Instead, be welcoming of their mistakes, guiding them gently as to how they can correct them with empathy. This is what validation gives them; a chance to get back up from their failures, learn from them, and try not to repeat them.

Validation versus Acceptance

Many parents confuse validating their child's behavior with accepting their behavior as correct. These aren't the same. Validation is simply to affirm the feelings of your child as something worth taking note of. You give their emotions the respect they deserve without brushing them off as inconsequential and meaningless. One of the biggest criticisms of the theory of empathy is that it encourages the child to feel confident about their mistakes and urges them to continue their bad behavior. This also isn't true.

Validation is not equal to condoning bad behavior. You are validating the way your child feels, but not the way your child behaves. While you are empathetic toward your child by telling them how you understand their feelings and as to why they are angry or upset, you also firmly establish how you do not support or condone their bad behavior. See the following as an example.

A three-year-old is upset that her older brother has finished her orange juice. They both get into an argument, and she throws the empty juice carton at her brother who ducks, and the empty box lands on the side table, holding crockery, breaking a glass quarter plate, and smashing it to pieces on the floor. Here their quarrel and argument have resulted in a broken plate and the danger of strewn glass pieces all over the kitchen floor. Any caregiver would be angry. She was in the right by being upset, but was the ensuing argument and throwing things appropriately? How must the parent react? How would you react?

What the child needs here is for us to understand that firstly she is simply three years old. Just two years older from being a no-idea-what's-happening infant. Only one year earlier from being able to talk. That is still a very young age for us to be taking them to the task. So, what do we do? What that child needs are a hug and a rub on the back that tells them you understand. If it is a sensitive child, they would be crying even before you look at them. A more hardened child is bound to melt into your arms and cry when you give that hug. Why is this so? Because at this tender age, kids are too innocent of fostering any real hatred or negativity. Their guilt will bring those tears on. At this point, they are overwhelmed by the loss of their juice and the loss of their own emotions. You would only be hurting them more by scolding or yelling at them.

Once they have calmed down, the crying has subsided, and they can look at you without being uncomfortable, now is the time to tell them it was wrong gently. By this time, they know that already. But you have to lay down the rules when your child is calm and in a receptive enough state to listen and acknowledge what you are saying.

"I know you were upset. You were angry; your brother drank your juice. But, dearest, what just happened wasn't fine. You mustn't throw things at each other. We talk about and solve our problems. We do not throw things at each other. That could have seriously hurt someone."

This much is enough to let the message sink in. But this message will only get in mind when you have held them and rubbed their backs, giving them that much-needed hug. That simple, empathetic gesture broke the barrier between the parent and the child. It is what made the child more accepting of their follies and the given advice. Of course, you mustn't forget the older brother or his part in this whole scenario, but for now, our concentration was the vulnerable little girl of three.

Validation is like saying I get how you are feeling. I don't agree with what you have done, but I understand why you have done it. You can and must set behavioral limits while being empathetic at the same time.

Strategies on How to Empathize with Your Toddler

If you are looking to be empathetic to your child's feelings, there are a few things to keep in mind to convey the right message of understanding effectively.

- Bring yourself to their level. Either bend down or kneel so that you both are at the same level.

- Look your child in the eye and truly listen to them. Put away any phones or electronics, or any other chore that you might be doing, to give them your undivided attention.

- Reflect and repeat what they say. It is always a good thing to happen what they tell you back to them. Doing this accomplishes two things. It tells them you have understood what they are saying and also opens for them a chance to correct you if you have in any way misunderstood them.

- Describe how they look and give those words to help them tell you how they feel. For example, you may say, "You are pounding the table with your fists; you look angry!"

- Ask them appropriate questions, so you know you are understanding them correctly and validating their feelings and not the souls you have chosen for them. For example, you might say something like, "You look sad, are you sad?" And then you let them agree or disagree.

Chapter 9: Let's Talk About Discipline

Discipline means to teach no punishment, but it also means solid clear limits and consequences for behaviors that are or can be dangerous (play with knives or sharp objects/ crossing the road, pushing others, etc.). For long-lasting behavior change.

The beginning of all effective discipline is parental self-control, thoughtfulness, and intention. At 12 to 18 months, when a child's ability to inhibit their behavior has not yet developed, there is no real necessity to discipline them for any reason. You can express boundaries and celebrate target behaviors—but scolding them for developmentally appropriate behaviors like wandering and mess-making should not be something a parent does at this stage. It is appropriate to prohibit certain behaviors by offering simple course correction or redirection, but anger about your child's poor self-control should be off the table.

Remember, discipline is much closer to the word "discipleship" than it is punishment. And yet, punishment is the word most parents closely associate with discipline. From zero to three years of age, it is especially important that we make sure all our discipline is rooted in teaching, connection, and care. During this time, while your child might be coloring on the walls and throwing food on the floor, make connection priority. Always share your expectations for their behavior in a way that expresses a benevolent understanding of both their limitations and their desires.

Effective Discipline vs. Punishment

Punishment has a punitive nature and does not change the behavior of a child. In many cases, punishment can even make the situation worse. The child only suffers and learns nothing. Unfortunately, punishment also tends to subject the child to humiliation, serious discomfort, anger, more frustrations, and anxiety, among others. On the other hand, effective discipline is both safe and healthy for the child. Although punishments are also used in an effective discipline strategy, such punishments are mild and only play a part of the whole strategy. Last but not the least, punishment controls a child while discipline guides a child, allowing him to learn from his mistakes and grow beautifully.

Say No to Spanking

Although spanking can be traced back to ancient times as a way to discipline a child, various studies today show that it is not effective. In fact, spanking can even make the situation worse. Spanking a toddler tends to make the child more aggressive, and it does not teach him the right conduct.

Spanking is based on pain. The theory behind it is that a person would not continue doing something that harms him. For example, if you touch a hot stove with your bare hands, you will get hurt, remove your hands immediately, and would no longer dare to do the same action again. Although this sounds logical enough, disciplining a child is not as simple as avoiding getting burned by a hot stove. When you discipline a child, you have not just tell the child what not to do but also what to do. Discipline teaches a toddler positive behaviors, which leads him to take positive actions.

Another thing that makes spanking harmful is that the child tends to lose trust in his parents. Your toddler looks up to you for support, comfort, and care. If you become a source of pain to them, especially if it happens a lot of times, then your child would tend to step back and put a shield around himself. This naturally damages the parent-child relationship.

If you are a parent who is used to spanking your child probably because that was how you were "disciplined" when you were young, or maybe because you simply thought it was the best way to save from child from being a bad person, here are five ways that you can do to stop yourself from spanking your child and be a better parent.

Learn to Use Words

Use words instead of physical aggression. Control yourself and talk calmly without scolding, and be sure to use words that your child can understand. Toddlers have a short attention span and cannot analyze things as good as adults, so keep your words short and simple. Since you communicate with words, you must also listen to your child. It should be a two-way conversation so that there will be understanding. It is also likely that there will be fewer problems if your child feels that you are listening to him. Just as you get exasperated when you feel that your child cannot understand what you are saying, your child also feels terrible when you do not listen to him.

Shift of Focus

Many times, all it takes is a shift of focus. Instead of focusing too much on the negative, focus on the positive behaviors. By giving all the time to positive things, there is no opportunity for the negative behaviors to even manifest themselves.

Let Him Learn On His Own

As people always say, "Experience is the best teacher." This is also true for toddlers. There are times that you do not have to spank your child just for him to learn. By simply letting the normal flow of things to unfold by itself, your toddler can learn from his own actions. For example, if he continues to play with his toy despite your warning roughly, the toy can soon break. This will teach your toddler a good lesson, which is more effective than simply spanking and hurting your child. But, of course, if there is a risk that is threatening to the life and well-being of your child, then you should intervene immediately and explain to your child the possible serious consequences.

Take a Timeout

Take a timeout. Except that this time, you should be the one who should take the timeout. Just before you lose your cool, give yourself a break. Step back for a minute and cool your temper. It is important to note that you should not face your toddler when you are not calm and centered. Unfortunately, if you are in a public place and you cannot step back and leave your kid alone, the best thing you can do is to pray and think of happy thoughts.

Have the Realization That Spanking Does Not Help

Time and again, various studies show that spanking is not a good way to discipline a child. In fact, spanking can only make things worse, and it does not make you a good parent. Therefore, instead of spanking your child, think of more ways that are positive and constructive on how you can correct the wrong behavior.

Four Pillars of Effective Discipline

The most effective techniques to discipline a child are characterized by four factors, which make them not only effective but also safe and healthy for the child. Unlike punishment, the four pillars of effective discipline promote childhood learning and welfare.

1) It builds a positive parent-child relationship

An effective discipline should be supportive of the relationship between the parent and the child. Unlike punishments that are based on fear, effective discipline is based on understanding, love, and support. You should keep in mind that toddlers are very sensitive, and their early childhood relationships have a great influence on their brain development, as well as on their behavior. By building up a positive relationship with your toddler, he will not only learn the right conduct but also enjoy a strong bond of love and trust with you.

2) It is safe

The safety of the child is of utmost importance. This is another reason why smart parents frown upon the use of punishments that involve bodily harm. Sometimes, the punishments can turn into cruelty and no longer serve the best interest of the child. Not to mention, many of such serious punishments are inflicted when the parent has already lost his patience and control of the situation.

3) It has reasonable expectations

Discipline teaches the child the right and proper conduct. Therefore, you should also consider the age and brain development of your child in making your expectations. Positive behaviors should be continuously enforced, while negative behaviors should be suppressed as early as possible. Be sure to take notice every time your child demonstrates good behavior, or at least try to do so.

4) It is composed of multiple techniques that are safe for the child

Effective discipline is a system of techniques or strategies. A certain technique is used depending on the situation. And, again, this pillar highlights the importance of the child's safety. Every challenging behavior should be taken as a learning opportunity, which can allow the child to learn and grow. As a parent, you must be able to approach the problem directly in a calm manner.

Is it Too late?

Some people think that it is too late to exercise discipline and that their toddlers can no longer change. It is worth noting that toddlers experience rapid changes. In fact, change is part of being a toddler. Either you turn a bad behavior into a good behavior, or let the bad behavior get worse. Of course, as a loving parent, you only want what is best for your child. So, if you are one of the many who think that it might be too late to begin using some discipline, then it should be clear to you by now that it is never too late to do so. Scientifically speaking, it is best to help your child grow in a positive light while he is still a toddler. If he gets to bring certain bad behavior up to his adulthood, they will be more difficult to correct.

What if It Does Not Work?

Another common dilemma shared by most parents is what if nothing changes even if they try to discipline their child? There are certain points to consider. First, there are many techniques that you can use to discipline your child. Second, you would not know if it will work unless you take the action to do so. Third, changing a bad or inappropriate behavior takes time and effort. Fourth, toddlers usually have more than a single behavior that you should try to improve. By applying a form of effective discipline, you can at least help him change some of his bad behaviors. If you are lucky enough, you might put right all his inappropriate manners. Fifth, exercising discipline increases the chances that your child will grow as a good person. Sixth, change happens not only in toddlers but also in adults. Therefore, there is no good reason to think that you cannot change your child's behavior. At the least, you can be able to teach him some good manners. Last but not the least, it is your responsibility as a parent to do everything for your child, to make him grow the best way you can.

All kids need boundaries. Boundaries are not only a great way to teach your toddler good behavior, but they also help him feel safe and secure. The tricky part about boundaries is setting and enforcing them. This becomes a little difficult, especially if you want to avoid bribing, threatening, or coercing your child to listen to you. You must be calm and set firm limits for your child. This is a simple exercise you must repeat time and again, without any inconsistencies. There are no timeouts when it comes to parenting - you are in it for the long haul.

Chapter 10: Taming Tantrum and Growth Spurts—A Toddler Style to Ask For Attention

Brain Development and Why it Matters

Cognitive, social, and emotional development between 12- and 36-months old children. What to expect?

	Brain Development	Social/Emotional Development
by 12 – 18 months	- Expresses 'no' - Expresses desire (i.e. through pointing) - Recognizes everyday concrete objects such as bottles, blankets, and books - Can follow single-step verbal commands such as 'sit down' or 'come here.'	- May begin to have temper tantrums - May begin to show a fear of strangers - Shows affection for others - May cling to mom, especially around strangers or in unfamiliar situations - Uses pointing to share interesting finds with others - Begins to explore by venturing out alone, usually as long as a caregiver/ parent is present

18 Months – 2 Years: Your little one is well into toddlerhood. By now, he is starting to speak in short sentences, show an increased interest in other children, engage in simple imaginative play, and follow more complex instructions. He can also recognize the names of objects or pictures of objects and point to them when prompted. By this age, he is able to experience the full range of emotions. Thanks to his burgeoning independence, more fully developed emotions, and lack of impulse control or emotional regulation, tantrums and refusals will begin to occur. Discipline strategies will continue to be focused on keeping your toddler safe and healthy while helping them to develop self-control. Check out the table below for a more in-depth look.

	Brain Development	Social/Emotional Development
by 2 years	- Points to things or pictures when they are named - Able to form short sentences (2-4 words) - Begins to be able to sort basic shapes and colors - Begins to play rudimentary make-believe games - Can follow instructions with two steps	- Mimics the words and behavior of others - Gets excited when around other children - Increases in independence - Shows defiant behavior - For the most part, plays next to other children rather than with them, but is beginning to include other children in simple games such as chase

2-3 Years: By now, your toddler is exhibiting increasingly complex cognitive abilities, including following more complicated instructions and completing simple puzzles. He is also able to hold short conversations with full sentences and demonstrates the enjoyment of and empathy for others. He's grown more socially independent, separating from parents with greater ease. The terrible twos have arrived full force, and you can expect more resistance when your toddler is tired or doesn't get his or her way. As with all stages of toddlerhood, discipline will continue to focus on health and safety, but now you can begin to introduce more concrete life skills such as sharing, turn-taking, and better emotional regulation.

	Brain Development	Social/Emotional Development
by 3 years	- Can follow instructions with 3 steps - Can hold a short conversation using 2 to 3 sentences - Can play with more complicated toys that include moving parts - Engages in imaginative play with people and toys - Can complete very simple puzzles	- Copies the behavior of others - Shows affection for others - Engages in turn-taking during games and other activities - Shows concern for friends or family in distress - Understands possession ('mine' vs. 'his' or 'hers') - Shows a wide range of emotions - Able to explore comfortably without a caregiver's presence, at least some of the time - May be upset or uncomfortable with changes in routine

3-4 Years: The skills that began to appear between 12 and 36 months will continue to develop, leading your toddler to be able to engage in more complex cognitive activities, such as memorizing nursery rhymes and beginning to conceptualize things like time and contrast. She may also show an awe-inspiring degree of creativity as she engages in imaginative play with herself, her toys, and others. By now, she's probably learned a degree of self-control when it comes to emotional regulation and is having fewer/shorter tantrums. She's made strides in impulse control, although it's still very much a work in progress. She has also learned to meet basic behavioral expectations, such as not throwing food, not hitting, and cleaning up toys. During this stage of development, discipline will become more focused on helping your toddler to learn the foundations of critical life skills such as cooperation and conflict resolution.

Age	Brain Development	Social/Emotional Development
by 4 years	- Abel to recite simple songs and poems from memory - Abel to tell stories and make predictions in a story - Understands the concept of counting and may be able to count - Begins to understand the concept of time - Understands the concept of 'same' and 'different.'	- Becomes increasingly creative with imaginative play - Enjoys playing with other children more than playing alone - Is able to cooperate with other children - Not always able to tell what's real and what's make-believe - Talks about likes and interests

As you can see, the toddler years are a crucial time for the brain and social development. As your child moves through each stage of toddlerhood, there some important supportive and risk factors to keep in mind to ensure your little one's optimal brain and social development.

Supportive factors are environmental, situational, and interpersonal influences that contribute to and/or support healthy development. Risk factors, on the other hand, may have an unhealthy, detrimental, or damaging effect on your child's brain and social/emotional development.

The table below lists some of the supportive and risk factors to look out for. Supportive factors should be encouraged within the home, and risk factors minimized or eliminated.

Supportive Factors	Risk Factors
- Responsive caregiver interactions (caregiver interprets and responds to toddler's emotions/needs in an accurate and timely manner) - Loving interactions - Hugs - Adequate nutrition - Healthy sleep - Time for safe exploration in a caregiver's presence - Structure and routine	- Lack of loving interaction from mother or primary caregiver - Invasive or unresponsive parenting - Too much 'screen time' - Poor nutrition - Poor sleep - Stress in the home - Abuse of the toddler - Abuse in the toddler's presence

Now that we've gone over some of the exciting developmental steps you can expect to see throughout toddlerhood, it's time to move on to the next aspect of our discussion on toddler discipline: Limits!

The Healing Power of Tantrums

What is a Tantrum?

Temper tantrums are frustrating. There is no way around it. However, they are not some majorly negative factors to consider—rather, they are learning experiences for everyone involved. Your child does not know better than to throw those tantrums. They happen when your child is feeling incredibly emotional, but is unsure about how to handle those big emotions that are roiling around inside him or her. For that reason, you should approach tantrums with grace and understanding—you should be willing and able to recognize that your child is not throwing this massive fit to hurt you, but rather because he or she feels entirely out of control.

Tantrums can range greatly from kicking and screaming to hitting or holding one's breath. Some children, particularly the stubborn ones, will hold their breaths until they finally end up passing out due to oxygen deprivation. While alarming to watch what happens at the moment, it is not putting your child at any real risk, and your child's body will take control before he or she can do any real, lasting harm.

Most often, these tantrums happen between the ages of 1 and 3. During this time, your child is going through a major period of development. Everything is new to your child—he or she may be learning how to interact with the world. There is the development of the concept of autonomy during this age as well—your child is finally beginning to recognize that he or she is their own independent person. Your child wants to interact and do so much, but they cannot communicate. They may want to impulsively do things that you know are harmful, such as jumping off of a counter, and when you stop them, they throw a fit. They cannot comprehend the reasoning behind why you say no at this point in time, and they find that they get overwhelmed by that frustration, disappointment, anger, or sadness that follows.

Reasons for Tantrums

Your Child Wants Something

Perhaps the most common reason for a tantrum is that your child wants something. They may want something that they cannot have at that moment, so they throw a big tantrum over it. Perhaps they want an ice cream cone for breakfast, but you know better, so you tell them no. They then throw a big fit because they are disappointed and angry.

Your Child Needs Something

Sometimes, the tantrum actually comes from an unmet need. They may be overly tired, overly hungry, thirsty, or need a diaper change. They need something and are struggling to communicate that need. If that need goes unmet due to not understanding it, the child may meltdown into frustration and tears.

Your Child Wants to Avoid Something

Sometimes, the tantrum is due to avoidance. You are trying to get your child to do something that he or she does not want to do, and instead of accepting that at face value, your child instead decides to cry and scream about it. For example, it may be bedtime, but your child is throwing a big tantrum about being put in the crib. Your child is looking for autonomy here and is attempting to assert his or her own will.

Your Child Wants Attention

Occasionally, if you have not been paying attention to your toddler and he or she wants your attention, a tantrum will arise. This is primarily due to the fact that toddlers operate under the assumption that even negative attention is better than no attention. If you have not been giving your child the attention that he or she needs and craves, you run the risk of having your child throw a tantrum just to get your eyes on him or her in the first place.

Your Child Can't Communicate

Sometimes, the tantrum comes down to just not being able to communicate wants and needs well. Your child has all of these big feelings that he or she has not yet learned to cope with, and because of that, they can become explosive.

Parent's Guide to Dealing with Tantrums

With those points in mind, you may be wondering how you can deal with tantrums as they arise. After all, ultimately, it will be your reaction to the tantrum that determines how the child learns to cope with them. You must be willing and able to regulate your own behaviors in order to ensure that, at the end of the day, your child learns how to self-regulate. You are setting the stage for whether your child learns that tantrums are acceptable, how to handle tantrums, or how to self-regulate. When you are dealing with a child that throws tantrums, try to remember the following:

1. **It is okay to be upset**: Remember, tantrums are not fun for anyone. It is normal that, at the sound of your child screaming, you feel stressed out. That is a normal biological reaction, and you are biologically predisposed to trying to make your child stop crying and screaming. Remember that it is a very normal reaction to be upset, but that being upset is not an excuse for you to lose your temper as well.

2. **Remember to take a deep breath**: Before you begin dealing with your child, try to practice the rule of stopping to take a big, deep breath. This will help you clear your own head and keep yourself from doing something that you will later feel guilty about or regret. You will also be teaching your child good self-regulation skills that will be developed further later down the line by showing him or her how you treat the situation.

3. **Remember that your child is having a hard time**: Many parents may find themselves asking why their children would do this to them. However, this is the wrong way to look at this situation. Your child is not trying to give you a hard time—he or she is having a hard time, and right at that moment, the only way that he or she knows how to deal with those big, strong emotions that are burning inside is through that tantrum.

4. **Stop to figure out why the child is throwing a tantrum**: If you know that your child regularly will have a tantrum when he or she is overtired, you can begin to avoid running into that problem. If you can identify common triggers for a tantrum, such as being hungry or tired, and it is a practical thing that you can avoid, you can make it a

point to avoid those pitfalls. If you know that your child gets overtired and throws fits when he or she skips naptime, you may make it a point to make naptime entirely sacred, and nothing short of an emergency will make you leave the house during that time.

5. **Don't be embarrassed**: If you have children, chances are, you have had a public tantrum at least once with your children present. If you have not, then your children are probably either too young to cause those sorts of tantrums, or your time is coming sooner rather than later. The vast majority of children will have some sort of public meltdown at some point over something—it is just a matter of time. This means that those parents around you know what you are going through. They know the frustration and anger that you are feeling. Don't be embarrassed if you get a rude stare or comment if your child throws a fit in public—it happens. It comes with the territory. Don't let other people distract you or make you feel bad, or you run the risk of otherwise struggling.

Redirection to tame tantrums

Perhaps one of the best skills that you have on you as a parent is the ability to redirect during a tantrum. This is particularly true when you are dealing with a child that is quite young—they are throwing a fit usually due to their emotional side of their brains being on auto-pilot at that point in time. Your child has the ability to think in a rational, calm manner, and an ability to think emotionally—we all have this. When the emotional side is running rampant and taking control of the situation, we are not making good decisions. We are acting in ways that are impulsive, and with that, impulsiveness often comes to all sorts of other problems as well. Our choices can wind up having all sorts of unintended repercussions that we were not ready to deal with.

If adults can fall for these same habits, then it should come as no surprise that your child can, as well. During these periods of time, when the child's emotions overwhelm him or her, they are unable to think with the rational parts of their minds. The emotional side has taken control during this time and is going to overwhelm their thought process and actions. This is exactly what happens in a tantrum. Your child is probably feeling some very big, very strong feelings that he or she does not know how to cope with, and because of that, he or she really struggles to make the proper progress needed to calm down.

When your child is mid-tantrum, however, you can usually re-engage with their logical side of their mind, pulling that back to the surface rather than allowing it to be stifled by emotional impulses. This is precisely what you will be doing when you are making use of redirection. You will be attempting to do or say something that will sort of cause the logical half of the child's mind to stop and pay attention—you want that logical half of the brain to reengage and control the individual.

Chapter 11: The Most Important Things Are Them Be Safe and Feel Loved, Not Well Behaved at All the Time

We are uncomfortable with our children's big emotions, particularly in public. We shame them; we belittle them, etc. It makes feel we are not doing a good job, but their brain still developing, it is normal that they will misbehave. We cannot control them, the environment, etc. If you want to control them all the time, you are breaking their will power. You break their joy.

Handling Behavior Problems

Children express their frustrations with various challenges through tantrums. Maybe your toddler is having difficulties in completing a specific task? Perhaps they don't have the right words to express what they feel? Frustrations play a major role in triggering anger that leads to tantrums. Let's look at various ways to handle tantrums in children.

Take the right steps to prevent the tantrums.

Schedule some frequent playtime with your little one. Allow them to choose the activity and make sure the child gets complete attention from you. Sharing a positive experience will offer your child an excellent foundation to calm herself down whenever they get upset. Check out the opportunities that will acknowledge her excellent performance. When a child receives favorable attention for the desired performance, they'll then form a habit of doing the same.

You can also create good tactics to deal with the frustrations immediately, like taking a deep breath. It's also essential to fess up after being angry over something. That's because your child needs to know it's OK to make mistakes once in a while. Make sure you know the things that lead to the tantrum and plan well. If the child gets frustrated when they're hungry, try to carry some healthy snacks. If the child starts grumbling when tired, try to make sleep time a priority.

Speak Whenever the Child Yells

Your toddler will match the tone of your voice since they want to get your attention. Bear in mind, and they're feeling angry and sad might assist you to remain calm. Whenever they lose control at a public spot such as the movies, take the child outside. Allow them to sit on the bench or in the car as they settle down. For most children, having such choices will help, mainly if the lack of control causes the outburst.

During a post-tantrum, try to follow through with the first demand that caused the outburst. If the child became frustrated because you asked them to collect the toy, they could still get it when they're calm. If the child started screaming because you didn't allow them to have a cookie, then give the cookie once they stop crying. When the child follows through and collects the toy, applaud the child. That's because it's a positive habit you'll want to instill in them.

Know Why Your Toddler Reacts Strongly

While your child can use words to express what they want, that doesn't imply that the tantrums have ended. They're still learning ways to handle emotions, and a slight disagreement will make them frustrated and sad. Since your toddler values their growing independence, requiring your help might be frustrating. They might break down when trying to complete a challenging task such as tying shoelaces and finds out they cannot do the job alone. Even though tantrums tend to start with anger, they're always deep-rooted in sadness. Children might get lost in how unjust and huge a situation becomes, so they struggle with how to do the task successfully.

Attempt this one tactic for tantrums for children under two and a half years. In most cases, children within this age bracket have 50 words in their vocabulary and can't link over two words together at a time. The child's communication is limited, but they have countless thoughts, needs, and wishes that must be met. When you fail to understand what they want, they tend to freak out to express their sadness and frustration. The remedy for this is to teach the children how to sign some words like milk, food, and tired. Empathizing with your child is another method to deal with outbursts. It assists in curbing the tantrums.

Give Your Child Some Space and Create a Diversion

In most cases, a child is supposed to get rid of the anger. So, just let them do it. This method will help your child know how to vent in a non-destructive manner. They'll have a chance to release their feelings, get themselves together, and recover self-control. Your child will engage in a yelling contest or fight with you. This approach can work in tandem with ignoring it a bit.

Chapter 11: The Most Important Things Are Them Be Safe and Feel Loved, Not Well Behaved at All the Time

This entails a definite mental switcheroo. Try to get your child engaged and interested in other things to make her forget about the bad experience. Make sure your backpack or purse has all kinds of distractions such as toys, comics, and yummy snacks. Once your child starts throwing tantrums, get the distraction out to catch your child's attention.

Note that a distraction can assist you in warding off a huge outburst before it occurs, provided you catch it in time. If you realize that your child is about to yell at the store since you don't want to buy them what they want, try to switch gears and enthusiastically say something such as, "Hey, do we need some bread. Do you want to assist me in getting a kind?" children tend to have a short attention duration, and this makes it easy to divert their attention. When doing this, make sure you sound psyched as it will make your child know it's real. They'll tend to forget about what made them feel sad and focus on the better things.

Offer a Big and Tight Hug

This might feel the hardest thing to do when your toddler is acting up, but it'll assist them to calm down. This should be a big tight hug and never say anything when doing it. Hugs will make your child feel secure and allow them to understand you care about them, even though you don't support the tantrum habits. In most cases, a child needs a safe place to release one's emotions.

Give Them Food or Suggest Some R&R

Getting tired and being hungry is the leading cause of tantrums in children. Since the child is on the brink emotionally, an outburst will quickly occur. Most parents keep wondering why their child has meltdowns that occur

during the same time every day—for instance, many toddler's tantrums
before lunch and in the evening, which is never a coincidence. If you're
experiencing this, make sure you feed your child well and give them enough
water. After that, let her veg, whether it involves taking her to bed or letting
her watch TV.

Give the Child Incentive to Behave

Some situations tend to be trying for children. They can encompass sitting
for long hours in a restaurant when eating or staying calm in church.
Irrespective of the scenario, the tactic is about noticing when you're asking
for too much from your child. Also, remember to give them the incentive for
the excellent work done. While heading to the restaurant, for instance, tell
her," Maya, mom wants you to sit and take your dinner nicely. I know you'll
do that! And if you behave well, you'll play your video games when we get
home. This type of bribery is perfectly provided. It's done as per your terms
and before time and not under pressure in the middle of a tantrum. In case
she begins to lose her temper, remind her about your promise. It's great how
it'll suddenly guide her back into shape.

Laugh it Off

As a parent, you fear public tantrums for various reasons. You're probably
afraid other people will brand you a bad parent, or that you're raising an out
of control child. However, that might lure you into making some choice that
will result in deep fits. Children are always smart, even the little ones. If you
get stressed and angry, allow them to find the best way to end the outburst

before many people begin staring, they'll learn on her own. The best thing is to suck it up, put on a smile, and pretend that everything is OK.

Get Out of That Place

Getting your little one away from the place of a tantrum will subdue the outburst. Additionally, it's an ideal strategy when you're in public places. When your child starts yelling over candy bars or a toy they want, take the child to a different place within the supermarket or even outside until they stop crying. Shifting the place will likely change the behavior.

Chapter 12: Tools for More Cooperative Children

Peaceful, Patient, and Positive Parenting

In certain situations, maintaining calmness, patience, and perseverance can be very difficult. However, it is possible. The only thing that gets in the way is how you, as a parent, look at your child's unpleasant behavior.

Children are small figures in an adult's world. Each of them is born with their own temperament and their right to choose what to do, whether it is useful or harmful to them. Since children speak in "other" languages, it is sometimes difficult for parents to understand them. From the parents' point of view, their little ones are too immature to make any decisions at all. However, it is true that, regardless of the consequences, children have the right to choose what they will do at certain times. You must be patient through this process. And that is not easy.

It's hard, but necessary to maintain calmness. If a parent thinks the child is "unresponsive" and that they "can't take the child's behavior anymore," then it is entirely normal for them to lose their patience, and in a large number of cases, lose control as well. Many parents then shout at the child in order to change the child's behavior.

A common feature that occurs in these cases is: Parents have lost their patience and lost their persistence.

However, if you step away from this unpleasant situation which makes you feel angry at your child, and you look at it objectively, you won't see the child's perspective as "insignificant" or see him as "misunderstood" but will see that he needs something. From this perspective, you can use logic and try to find out exactly what your child needs and what you need to do to help him. So, as you do this, you are constantly and patiently "reading" your child.

So, What is Patience?

Being a persistent and patient parent means putting in consistent and constant work to develop quality and constructive communication with your child because you must reach your child's inner self and feelings. One of the positive side effects that you will achieve as an efficient parent is that with all of your patience and understanding as you manage the child's behavior and help them, one day, your toddler becomes an emotionally intelligent and responsible person.

The essence of positive discipline is to learn to change yourself instead of trying to change others and to make others want to change. If you're busy trying to control your child, you are not thinking about the ability to solve problems by controlling your behavior and making decisions about your actions, rather than trying to correct your child's behavior.

It is easy to fall into the temptation to repeat what you have said, to remind the child of something, and to explain it instead of just doing what you have already told. Careful and resolute parenting gives parents the opportunity to spend time developing the great features that their child possesses, talks with them on many interesting topics, and giving them an explanation of how things work in life.

Punishment: Toughness through Love. Should I Punish a Child?

Apparently, most parents think you should punish a child. But it is important to define the concept of "punishment." Punishment can be a strict tone in your voice, temporarily depriving the child of positive interaction, sweets, or any privileges that are reserved for obedient children.

We don't even contemplate using physical punishment, and when parents have outdated ideas about the admissibility of corporal punishment, we hope that they can be immediately corrected!

Of course, it's hard to imagine a mother who has never raised her voice in her life. But we can imagine the surprise of an angry mother when in response to a slap her own child turns around and does the same thing!

If you punish children physically, you risk making them angry, and depending on the individual characteristics of their personality; they will not only remember everything in detail but may also want to get revenge!

Imagine a situation where the child doesn't think about the consequences of his actions or forgets what you have told him earlier. Even if the child did something deliberately disobedient, do not lower yourself to his level, and respond in kind. Be patient, and be wiser.

Punishments Don't Help Much

If we take into account that the punishment causes a negative emotional state and causes the child to feel embarrassed, frightened, and insecure, we can understand that punishment does not motivate the child to learn from the situation. That is why it is useful for parents to make a decision about what their parenting goal is: absolute obedience or a relationship of trust.

What Punishment Can Do?

Punishment implies a loss of opportunity for experiential learning, but also causes a loss of opportunity to create a relationship of trust between you and your child. If the child fears punishment, he will not feel encouraged to learn, to draw conclusions, and later to develop responsibility.

How to Replace Punishment with Positive Parenting

A positive approach to parenthood implies an understanding of the child and of his or her behavior, paying attention to how the child feels. What does that mean practically? Seeing what is behind a child's behavior means seeing the real cause, understanding it, and offering the child an alternate solution to negative behavior.

Adults mostly only see the "final product"—the unwanted behavior that they want to correct, or a symptom of the real cause. If they want the child to learn something and that isn't working, it is up to adults to explain to the child the consequences of his negative behavior: Natural consequences ("You are cold because you do not want to wear a sweater.") and logical consequences ("We are late for the birthday party because you wanted to play even though the clock was ringing and telling us it was time to go.").

Positive parenting creates a space for learning without guilt, shame, and the fear of punishment.

Children learn by making a series of efforts and mistakes. The whole process of a child's upbringing and learning is a series of attempts and mistakes until they master some skills. The role of the parents in this process is to provide direction and leadership. You must be a teacher to your children first of all, but a patient one.

The part of the brain that is responsible for reason, logic, and the control of impulses is not fully developed until adolescence. "Immature" behavior is normal in "immature" human beings that have "immature" brains. This is a scientific fact, and whatever you feel as a parent, and however you behave in these situations, you will not change that.

Parenting is difficult and requires the patience to repeat the same thing hundreds of times. Being a child is also difficult because it requires strength and persistence to repeat the same thing hundreds of times until it is learned. This process cannot be accelerated, skipped, or eliminated. The only thing a parent can do is change their perspective and accept that some things are slow and annoying, and have to be repeated many times. Some parents have days when they feel discouraged because they have to repeat the same thing day after day. But that is also a great part of parenthood.

Children learn about the world from their parents, and learning isn't just about gathering information. One of the most important things in your child's process of learning is learning how to live in the society in which he or she is growing up and learning the rules to function in that society. Kids have to know when it is proper and better for them to limit their autonomy and self-expression, and they have to know that they are able to do it. Then, they have to learn how to tolerate frustration and handle frustration and to be consistent in spite of it.

If we allow them to, children will try to solve the problems they face in their development and upbringing. Parents often begin to scold or criticize the child, not expecting the child to attempt to solve the problem. If the parents were more patient, they would be surprised how much their children are actually capable of making conclusions and solving the problems they face.

Being heard is therapeutically powerful and allows us to think about things clearly and find a solution. The same goes for children. Sometimes it's enough just to listen to a child when they talk about the problems they are having because they often come up with solutions that resolve the problems.

Fear and control are effective in the short term, but a child can become either completely blocked in his development or can begin to provide resistance to parental pressure through defiance and rebellion. Depending on the type of interaction a child has with his or her parents, the child forms a picture of himself and a sense of self-reliance in his roles in life. A blocked, non-progressing child has a lesser perception of his value, which can lead to isolation or to its opposite: aggressive and rebellious behavior.

Children should understand the importance of thoughts and emotions, not just behavior, because it will enable them to function better in relationships with other people and to deal better with problems. That is why adequate control of their emotions is an important skill and one of the most important goals of parenting.

The words of parents and their assessments of a child are a mirror for that child. Children will see what their parent's exhibit. That then becomes their picture of themselves, and they live with that. That is why it is very important to be specific and accurate with criticism. Criticism should be expressed with body language, which expresses regret rather than disapproval toward the child. A parental look full of condemnation and criticism will be internalized by the child, and we want to love and accept our children. This strong support for them will be the seed and the core of their happy life and success.

However, you shouldn't give your child unlimited freedom; you do need to discipline them, of course. But, how? Disciplinary measures respond to the child and his abilities and support the child in developing self-discipline. Discipline aims to positively target children, recognizing individual values, and building positive relationships. Positive discipline empowers children's faith in themselves and their ability to behave appropriately.

Discipline is training and orientation that helps children to develop limits, self-control, efficiency, self-sufficiency, and positive social behavior. Discipline is often misunderstood as punishment, especially by those who apply strict punishment in their endeavors to make changes to children's behavior. But discipline is not the same as punishment.

Chapter13: Take a Deep Breath and Self-Regulate (As for Everything in Life)

Slow down against your impulse to get irritated. Become present, look at your child, and connect.

Many parents attest to the reality that disciplining a toddler is like facing constant uphill battles. These little bundles of delight can turn to extremely stubborn kids who test the patience limits of caregivers and adults around them.

It is also the phase of childhood where they begin to assert their independence. One of their first words is "No," affirming the toddlers' love to do things in their way. They enjoy running away to escape. Normal toddlers are full of energy. They run, jump, play, explore, and discover everything that interests them. They love to use the sense of touch, exploring things with their senses. Because toddlers are easily stimulated by what they see or hear, their impulsive nature can make them clumsy and touch things. Parents need to teach their children safe ways to touch or handle things and not to touch hot objects.

Although raising a toddler entails a lot of hard work, seeing your child grows and develops his skills is fascinating. However, because of the developmental changes that rapidly happen during the toddler stage; it is necessary to use a disciplinary approach that will foster the child's independence while teaching him socially appropriate behavior and other positive traits.

All too often, there is an assumption that parenting techniques apply to all, and kids will react or respond in a similar pattern. But every child has his own set of traits. They are in his DNA, which he inherited from his parents. Some toddlers are shy or even-tempered, while others are outgoing and have aggressive natures.

By understanding the child's special personality and natural behavior, you can help him adjust to the real world. It is necessary to work with his personality and not against it, taking into account the following factors that you need to consider when disciplining your toddler. Giving proper care and nourishment, providing positive and healthy activities, and instilling positive discipline is vital to his physical, mental, emotional, social, and behavioral growth…

Temperament and Behavior

Temperament is defined as the heritable and biologically based core that influences the style of approach and response of a person. The child's early temperament traits usually predict his adult temperament.

The child's behavior is the outcome of his temperament and the progress of his emotional, cognitive, and physical development. It is influenced by his beliefs about himself, about you, and the world in general. While it is inborn and inherent, there are certain ways to help your toddler manage it to his advantage.

Nine Dimensions or Traits Related to Temperament

1. The activity level pertains to the amount of physical motion that your toddler demonstrates, while engaged in some activities. It also includes his inactive periods.

- Is your child a restless spirit who cannot sit still for so long or want to move around?

- Is your toddler the quiet, little one who enjoys playing alone or watching TV?

2. Rhythmicity refers to the predictability or unpredictability of physical and biological functions which include hunger, bowel movement, and sleeping.

- Does your child thrive on routine and follow regular eating or sleeping patterns?

- Does he display unpredictable behavior and dislike routine?

3. Attention span and persistence are the skills to remain focused on the activity for a certain period.

- Does your toddler stick to complete a task?

- Is he easily frustrated and look for another activity?

4. Initial Response (Approach or Withdrawal) refers to the reaction to something new and unfamiliar. It describes his initial feelings to a stimulus like a new person, place, toy, and food. His reaction is shown by his mood or facial expressions like smiling or motor activity, such as reaching for a toy or swallowing food. Negative responses include withdrawal, crying, fussing, pushing away, or spitting the food.

- Is he wary or reluctant around unfamiliar situations or strangers?

- Does he welcome new faces and adjust comfortably with new settings?

5. The intensity of the reaction is associated with the level of response to any event or situation. Toddlers respond differently to events around them. Some shrieks with happiness or giggle joyfully, others throw fits, and many barely react to what is happening.

- Do you always experience trying to guess the reaction of your child over something?

- Does your child explicitly show his emotions?

6. Adaptability is the child's ability to adjust himself to change over time.

- Is your child capable of adjusting himself to sudden changes in plans or disruptions of his routine?

- Does he find it difficult to cope up with changes and resist it as much as he can?

7. Distractibility is the level of the child's willingness to be distracted. It relates to the effects of an outside stimulus on your child's behavior.

- Can your child focus on his activity despite the distraction that surrounds him?

- Is he unable to concentrate when there are people or other activities going on in the environment?

8. Quality of mood is related to how your child sees the world in his own eyes and understanding. Some react with acceptance and pleasure while other children scowl with displeasure just "because" they feel like it.

   - Does he display mood changes constantly?

   - Does he generally have a happy disposition?

9. Sensory Threshold is linked to sensitivity to sensory stimulation. Children who are sensitive to stimulation requires a careful and gradual introduction to new people, experiences, or objects.

   - Is your child easily bothered by bright lights, loud sounds, or food textures?

   - Is he totally undisturbed with such things and welcome them as such?

There are three main types of toddlers:

1. Active or Feisty Toddlers—These children have a tremendous amount of energy, which they show even while inside the uterus of their mothers, like lots of moving and kicking. As an infant, they move around, squirm, and crawl all over the place. As toddlers, they climb, run, jump, and even fidget a lot to release their energy. They

become excited while doing things or anxious around strangers or new situations.

They are naturally energetic, joyful, and loves fun. But when they are not happy, they will clearly and loudly say it. These toddlers are also quite obstinate and hard to fit in regular routines.

To help him succeed:

- Acknowledge his unique temperament and understand his triggers.

- Teach him self-help skills to get going if his energy is low or how to calm down when his activity level is very high. Some simple and effective ways to calm down are counting from 1 to 10, taking deep breaths, doing jumping jacks to get rid of excess energy, and redirecting him to other activities.

- Set a daily routine that includes play and other activities that enhance his gross motor movements. Provide him with opportunities to play and explore safely. It is necessary to childproof your home.

- Insist on nap time. An afternoon nap will refresh his body and mind, preventing mood swings and tantrums.

- Do not let him sit in front of a television or do passive activities. Break the boredom by taking him outside and play in the outdoors.

- Become a calming influence. Understand how your temperament affects his temperament and find ways to become a role model.

2. Passive or Cautious Toddlers- These children prefer activities that do not require a lot of physical effort, move slower, and want to sit down more often. They are slow-to-warm-up when meeting new people and often withdraw when faced with an unfamiliar situation. They also need ample time to complete their tasks.

To help him succeed:

- If your child is less active, set guidelines or deadlines that will prompt him to finish the given tasks.

- Invite him to play actively by using interesting noises, bright toys, or gentle persuasion.

- Always accentuate the positive. Be generous with praise and words of encouragement when they display efforts or achieve simple milestones.

3. Flexible or Easy Toddlers - These children are very adaptable, generally calm, and happy. But sometimes, they are easily distracted and need a lot of reassurance and love from you.

To help him succeed:

- Be realistic and expect mood changes when something is not smooth-sailing. Do not be too hard on the child when he displays unusual outburst.

- Provide him with interactive activities and join him. Sometimes, it is easy to let him play his own devices because of his good-natured personality. It is necessary to introduce other options to enhance his skills.

- Read the signs and find out the reasons for subtle changes in the behavior and attitude toward something. Be observant and have a special time for him.

Chapter 14: Coach: State What Is Going on

Most of the time, there are underlining reasons for your child's uncooperative behavior; you are anxious, you are rushing, and you are suffering, and their pick on that. Reclaim that connection. Try to be funny about, get silly. Let go a bit of control if it is a minor issue.

If it does not work, comment that 'you are having a difficult time this morning. It's ok you don't want your shoes on' agree that is not put the shoes on, put them in your bag and try to break the drama by singing a favorite song, get silly, etc..

You need to act big ONLY when is actually needs it: stop at the end of the pavement, do not run into the road, etc.

How You Affects Toddlers

For kids, their parents are the live example and guideline. The very first role model of a kid is his or her mother and father. The kids observe how their parents are dealing with the people, issues, matter, and routine work as well. Other than the actions, your traits and personality do affect the kid and a kind of model for them.

Before getting started with how your personality affects theirs, it is necessary to know what defines your personality. Personality is the combination of behavior, reaction, treatment to the situation, and public dealing. If, as a parent, you are kind to others and have a polite nature, the kid will learn the politeness and kindness through observation. Same as on the other hand, if you have anger issues or are mostly confused in the decision making or taking a stance, then your child will end up with the same condition.

When it comes to making your kid learn the positive discipline, you need to work on the overall discipline as well. Something you want your kids to learn, you are supposed to do the same in front of them. As per the recent study of behavioral learning explains that kids are good at observation, and the visuals they have in daily life are the biggest source for them to learn everything. From the manners to behaviors and even the way of life, they learn from the environment and elders.

Watch Your Actions

If you want to bring change in your kid, the most important thing is to watch your actions. If you are lying to your kids, they will lie back to you. This is something that is learning from your behavior and action in the first place. You are supposed to give them reasons for everything that is happening.

Do Not Find the Easy Escape

Scolding a child on questions, giving lame excuses, or ignore their questions is the easy escape that parents have most of the time. This is something that can lead to adverse behavioral changes in the kids. They will adopt the habit of ignorance and anger when they are unable to sort out the problem or do not have answers.

Make Them Reasoning

If there is something you are unable to do for the kids, or some things are impossible or unmanageable, then you are supposed to reason that. When you give solid and measurable reasons for something that develop a habit and understanding of logic in the kid, they will know the way to say not is proper reasoning, not just running away. It seems to be a difficult task in the beginning, but eventually, you can make some real improvements in your kid's behavior and overall discipline as well.

Understanding Developmental Appropriateness

Developmental appropriateness is an approach to teach the kid. In this approach, the curriculum is designed according to age and individual needs. The basic objective of this program is that every kid fits in this program. In other words, it is a program for each kid. He should not need to fit in the program as the program will fit in him.

Best Curriculum Design Strategy

Designing the curriculum for preschoolers is a critical task. A teacher needs to keep various elements in mind. The appropriate development strategy helps the teacher to design the best curriculum concerning this approach curriculum designed according to the capabilities of a student. At a certain age, what he can do physically, cognitively, and emotionally. This strategy helps in all these perspectives.

Every Children's Need is Different

The teachers of preschool look at the whole child individually. They see his physical, intellectual, emotional, social, and creative growth. The growth of these different segments raised in every child at its speed. Some factors developed in some children at an early stage. On the other side, in some children, they develop later.

Every child has capabilities, but teachers need to recognize and polish them. Some preschoolers have strong intellectual skills. But he needs to develop those skills through socialization. Likewise, some kids have great speaking power. However, the only thing they need is the confidence to speak in public. Besides this, some common developmental patterns are there, too, the same for all kids.

Role of a Teacher

Through the developmentally appropriate approach teacher observe all the preschooler's behavior. By utilizing her experience, she will recognize the capabilities of students. According to their strength, teachers design and plan the activities. She tried that those activities should not be too easy or too tough for kids. The purpose of these activities is to help students to grow and learn.

Flexible Method

To make it feasible for all the student's development appropriate approach has flexible methods. These methods are open-ended and have limited chances of mistakes. The reason behind this strategy is to teach all the kids equally. With the fewer chances of mistakes, students learn with confidence.

Students Keep Themselves Active

For a child's positive discipline, he must remain busy in positive activities. The development appropriation keep

The kid busy. If your preschooler is engaged in his independent activities, it is a sign. Yes, it is a sign of his appropriate development. He will not get frustrated or bored, rather than that, he will engage in the activities his teacher taught him.

The Miraculous Brain: In learning and Development

Your child has a miraculous brain like other kids. Even before birth till age 5, the child's brain develops with the highest speed. Brain development at an early age has a long-lasting impact on his ability to learn. This early learning remains with him for the rest of his life. His early childhood's positive or negative experiences play a key role in his brain development.

Strong Observation

The observation of a child at an early age is very strong. His brain picks up the information and actions at an incredible pace. His brain process that observation speedily, and he connects all his observations with observations.

He observes people around him and their behavior towards them. Along with this, he observes his physical environment, for instance, colors, food, fabric patterns, sounds, roof, walls, and so on. These observations play an important role in his early development and learning.

Strong Five Senses

The miraculous brain keeps all his five senses super active. His listening, speaking, seeing, tasting, and touching; all senses are really strong at this age. From a normal person, their brain absorbs more than these senses. His senses make him extra sensitive, especially about his physical environment. With these multiple strong senses, he learns various things in a short time.

Learn to React

As a child's brain works efficiently, he learns to react. Since the birth of a child, he starts his journey to learn how to react. When he should laugh or cry. How to tell he is hungry or in pain? He starts to understand the feelings of joy or sadness.

Similarly, he reacts to the situations. He learns who is her mother or to whom he feels protective? He learns all these reactions and feelings at high speed through amazing brain functions.

The Growth of Child's Brain Ability

According to the studies, initial years are really important for a kid's learning. You are thinking about how he digests lots of information at the same time. Yes, you are thinking right because adults, mostly can't digest more information at a time. But a kid's brain works differently. You will be surprised by the kid's brain ability development process.

A kid's brain ability not decreased but increased with increasing information. With the increased information, he started to connect and relate it with the information. It expands his imagination and learning canvas.

Excellent Memory

At an early stage of life, a kid has an excellent memory. He observes things and saved them in his brain. He tried to copy the actions of the people around him. Most of the kids didn't forget anything that they see only once. Therefore, parents need to behave well when kids are around them.

Strategies to Enhance Brain Function in Learning and Development

As mentioned earlier, every child has a miraculous brain. But the pace of learning of each child will be different from others. If you feel that your kid is going at a slow pace, don't worry. You and her teachers can deal with it. Some strategies will enhance his brain function to help him.

Active Their Mind

If you see your kid is not properly acting, help him in activating his mind. You can do this by engaging him in different healthy physical activities. These activities must be interesting and should be designed according to the kid's age. I must try to make them not too simple or too hard. Talk to his teacher and design an activity jointly so that he can do this in school and at home.

Social Gatherings

Man is a social animal and can't live without others. Similarly, kids also need to socialize for their development and mental growth. Take them to the parks and allow them to socialize with the kids. It will help them to make friends. On the other hand, his sadness or depression will vanish. You will observe the positive change in your kid's behavior with this simple action.

Besides eliminating his sadness, he will learn positive discipline. He will learn to share, cooperate, and to help others. In schools, teachers arrange parties or social gatherings just because of its positive impact.

Deal Him According to His Age

You need to deal with the child according to his age. If he is three years old and you feel he is weak in counting. Don't worry. Just leave him for some time. Four years is the age when a child's brain cortex is formed. That's the point that you were looking for. It is best for mathematics and logic.

At this age, gently start to encourage him to count. Give him small activities like collecting the objects. Likewise, labeling and comparing different objects. Teach him while playing. Don't force him and don't get angry. He will sometimes learn within minutes or sometimes within days.

Be Gentle

For kid's brain development and learning, your anger can be destructive. Kids only need your attention and love, whether you are a parent or teacher. Kids are sensitive in nature; thus, handle them with care and be gentle. It is possible he will take some time to learn, but it's ok. He is a child. Put yourself in his position or level and see what you will do?

Chapter 15:How to Agree With Your Partner and Other Carers

The same process, connect with yourself, express empathy for their points, and say that you hear them and their concerns. How were you parented, and what you wish your parents did differently?

Communication is Vital

Communication is critical in any relationship, and the one you have with your baby is no different. The period from ages 1 through 4 is vital to your toddler's emerging language and social skills. Parent-child communication during this stage of development is all about effective interaction, modeling communicative behaviors, and fostering confidence, safety, and self-development.

The first thing to remember about communicating with your toddler is that it is a dynamic, two-way interaction. One reaches out, the other response. As you and your toddler learn to interact in increasingly responsive and effective ways, he will develop an increased sense of safety, confidence, empathy, and self-determination.

Let's consider some of the critical components of effective communication.

Effective Communication: Talking

The way that a parent speaks communicates much more than mere words. When you engage verbally with your toddler, you are modeling how a conversation works, including relevant skills such as listening, empathy, and turn-taking. As toddlers observe you talking to themselves and others, what they learn about human interaction contributes to their understanding of what it means to communicate effectively and exist in a social context.

But setting a good example isn't the only thing to keep in mind. The way that parents speak to their toddlers also impacts how effective the communication is (does the toddler understand in an actionable way?) and the toddler's developing emotional and social understanding.

Talking to your toddler in ways that are too aggressive or too passive can have negative consequences on their emotional and social development as well as detract from the potential benefits of teaching moments and healthy discipline. Instead, parents should speak firmly but kindly as they seek to communicate with their toddlers.

With these essential points in mind, let's consider some vital tips in talking in ways that your toddler can understand:

Use eye contact. When talking with your toddler, don't expect them to listen or know if you're just talking at them. Set aside any distractions, make eye contact, and let yourself connect fully with your little one.

Eye contact will help your toddler to pay attention to what you're saying and stay engaged in the conversation. It will also help bolster their sense of personhood by making it clear that you are interested in them.

Speak to them by name. Using your toddler's name while talking with them is another way to keep them focused on the conversation and give them a sense of importance as a co-communicator. It's especially useful to use names when validating or trying to let them know that you approve or disapprove. For example, 'Wow Jonny, that sounds so frustrating,' or 'I love how you shared with your sister, Alex,' or 'We don't throw food, David—please stop.'

Don't yell. Once you start yelling, the chances are that your toddler's behavior will become worse, either right then and there, or manifested tomorrow or a week. Yelling sets a poor example for your toddler and is likely to cause them stress that could become damaging. You may also frighten them, further adding to their anxiety and fueling further misbehavior as they try to cope. Instead, speak in a calm but firm voice. If needed, take a moment to breathe and calm down before speaking.

Be assertive but not aggressive. Be clear about the purpose of your communications by using a confident tone and body language when appropriate. However, do not mistake assertiveness for aggression. Assertiveness effectively communicates ideas and expectations; aggressiveness expresses anger, fear, and dislike.

Smile. Babies and toddlers are particularly responsive to facial expressions. As you undoubtedly discovered during the first year, sometimes a well-directed smile is all that it takes to brighten up a sad baby. The same holds for toddlers. Offering smiles during a conversation, let your toddler know that you enjoy talking with them and that the conversation is meant to be fun.

Minimize the use of 'no.' while some limits will undoubtedly focus on what your toddler should do, many will focus on what they should not do. Hearing 'no' over and over again throughout the day can be exhausting for your little one. Try to talk to him in favorable terms that model reasoning.

For example, instead of saying 'No Michal! Don't throw your food,' you might try 'Hmmm, throwing our food makes the floor sticky. Let's try saving it for later instead.'

Don't talk too much. When speaking, keep it simple. Toddlers have short attention spans, and talking too much will likely cause your toddler to lose interest. For example, one day, 2-year-old Jimmy threw his toy car straight at the window. His mom responded by saying, 'Now Jimmy, you can't throw your toy car at the window because if you end up breaking the window we're going to have to buy a new one, and that costs a lot of money, and besides, throwing things is dangerous—what if you hurt someone? How do you think it would feel? Do you think it's nice to…' at this point, Jimmy has stopped tracking? His mother is using too many words, discussing people that aren't even present, and speaking in terms that a 2-year-old can't follow or relate to. Instead, she might say something like, 'Jimmy, don't throw your toys in the house. Throwing is for outside.' At two years of age, short, direct explanations of not more than 2-3 sentences are the most likely to result in understanding.

Use good manners. Using 'please' and 'thank you' will model proper behaviors for your toddler and help her see that kids and adults alike deserve respect in a conversation.

Ask questions. Asking open-ended questions is a great way to show interest in your toddler and encourage participation in the conversation. When trying to promote interaction, avoid problems that can answer with a short yes/no. Instead of asking, 'Did you go to the park with Grandma?' question, 'What did you do at the park?'

Don't limit the conversation to directions. Finally, don't just use talk to give your little one direction or feedback. Their language skills are growing a mile a minute at this age, and they are learning that language can use for all kinds of purposes. To support this growth and create positive interaction patterns by asking them about their day, their opinions, asking them to tell stories, solve problems out loud, etc. Responses will be limited at first, but need not be any less enjoyable. You will be astounded by how quickly your toddler's language develops in just a few short years.

Effective Communication: Listening

Listening goes hand in hand with talking. It's challenging to do one effectively without the other. Being a good listener will encourage your toddler to talk and help them develop excellent communication skills. Remember, effective communication with your toddler is dynamic and interactive, which means modeling both talking and listening abilities.

Listening serves several communicative purposes, including gathering information, opening the door for empathy, building relationships, giving respect, and gaining perspective. Listening will help you to understand what is going on in your little one's mind and heart, letting you relate to them better as you help them solve problems.

> **Tip 1: Ask for details**. When your toddler tells you about what happened at church or that her baby doll feels sad, show that you are listening by asking for more information. What happened first? Second? Third? Why is the baby doll sad? How will you make her happy? In addition to showing that you are listening and interested, such questions elicit a new language and help your toddler to practice

critical cognitive functions such as recall, mental modeling, and problem-solving.

Tip 2: Pay attention. In today's world, multitasking has become a way of life, even when it's unnecessary. Show your toddler that you're listening and engaged, set aside devices such as phones or tablets, and give them your full attention.

Tip 3: Use active listening. Active listening refers to listening that is purposeful and fully engaged. During active listening, you entirely focused on what is said. Body language cues, including eye contact, mirroring facial expressions, and an attentive posture, all contribute to active listening. When you listen actively, your toddler will be more likely to feel that what they have to say is essential, and they will be encouraged to speak more.

Tip 4: Be physically interactive. High fives, hugs, and gestures are all great ways to show that you are listening and interested in what your toddler is saying. Getting bodies involved will also make the conversation more engaging and meaningful.

Tip 5: Give unconditional love. Toddlers seriously lack impulse control and often don't know how to express themselves in socially appropriate ways. They may speak out of anger and even say things like 'I hate you' or 'You're ugly.' Remember, don't take it personally! No matter how your toddler speaks to you or what the content of their message is, make sure that they always know that you love them, no matter what. Unconditional love creates a safe space where toddlers can speak freely and make mistakes without fear of losing your love or affection. This freedom will do wonders for their language skills, confidence, and trust in you as a parent.

How to deal with "I don't want..."

Chapter 16: How to Coach Siblings' Relationship and Rivalry

Fights with Siblings

Siblings fighting with each other is another day-to-day experience a parent should expect. Fights can happen for literally any reason at all; kids can fight over toys, kids can fight for space, fights can even occur over who sits on daddy's lap, whatever it is, kids can fight over it.

Fights, sometimes, can be intentionally sparked by one child or the other; children can seek attention by any means possible, even if it is negative, and after all, half bread is better than none. Competition is another reason why siblings fight each other; fights can happen over who does what first, first to have a bath, who gets dressed first, until the end of the world, kids will compete and fight for supremacy. In the twinkle of an eye, playtime can turn into wartime between siblings.

Having a younger sibling can be frustrating for a toddler, which would cause them to express their anger by trying to start a fight. A toddler is yet to understand what it means to have a younger one; all he knows is that one new little creature has come to hijack all the attention, love, and care he's been getting.

It's not an easy job for a parent who, by the addition of a new member into the family, now has to add refereeing to the long list of parental tasks. In fact, some parents find it hard to the extent that they never even know what to do when the war begins, this war which happens, at least, about six times a day. The following are some tips that should be taken for the tackling and reduction of the daily inevitable sibling squabbles.

- **Kids learn from what they see**: Make sure you are not just telling your kids to do as you say, behave how you want them to copy; when your kids see that you handle everything that comes your way aggressively, you are only teaching them to be aggressive as well, how they see you treat and relate to people matters a lot, the kind of relationship they notice between you and your partner is another example they will learn from.

- **Calmness in intervention**: When fights erupt, and you want to intervene, be sure to show a high level of calmness; yelling never solves anything; it only brings about escalation; I know it is really annoying to see your kids getting in a brawl, but be sure to suppress your anger and not show your frustration.

- **Try not to judge and take sides**: When you hear your kids fighting over something (probably a toy), and you get there, with or without an idea of who had it first, try settling the fight regardless, putting blames can build grudges in the Kids' minds. It's normal to think about fairness, but trust me; the other kid will have the fault too some other time; there you have your balance.

- **Ignorance**: This will be needed at some point, when you find out that your kids start to fight in search of attention, then some amount of ignorance will help make them know that negative attention is not a way of life, because if they are always getting it anytime they fight, then they will keep on doing it anytime attention is needed. Well, a great way to prevent this is to make sure kids have a lot of equal time and attention.

- **Assurance of importance**: This is for an older toddler who is having a younger sibling, they believe that with the arrival of the new little one, their significance goes down the drain, they will do almost anything to make sure that doesn't happen; they'll fight for their right. This also requires a lot of attention to the older toddlers so that they can feel secure and not feel threatened by the arrival of the new one. Parents can prevent this by preparing the kid for the new baby, you create a connection even before the baby is born, having them talk to the baby, feel the baby kick, see images of the baby in the belly, can create the desired connection, making them through pictures of their baby days can also help prepare them for what is coming.

- **Verbal lessons**: Try explaining to your kids how bad it is to fight their siblings, show them how they can live together in peace and harmony; you can even encourage them to employ turn-taking; it helps reduce the rate of fighting as they know they will have their turns.

Fights Over the Table

Your toddler frequently gives you a hard time each mealtime; this can happen as a result of a variety of reasons. Below is a list of possible causes of toddlers' mealtime fight and their respective solutions.

- **You show too much attention**. When you concentrate too much on your kid at mealtime, showing too much concern about how much they eat, showing excitement when they eat well, or displeasure when they eat less. It puts pressure on them, which displeases them, and in turn, they lose interest, then the war begins.

- You can give them some amount of freedom and a sense of independence at mealtime. When they feel they are in control, then they don't get to feel that eating is an obligation.

- **Transition problem**. You have to work the transition into them before time; notifying them beforehand is essential so that when the time finally comes, they will be prepared. For example, when it's about ten minutes before mealtime, you say to them, "Amber, you have eight minutes until mealtime, you'll need the two minutes extra time.

- **Tiredness**. Kids, after so much unrest, become too tired to do anything, and yes, they can also be too tired to eat. Be sure to plan your kids' daily schedule well, with a balanced amount of rest and activity so that they don't eventually become over-worked or stressed out.

- **Snack, eaten too close to mealtime**. When your kid has a satisfying snack too close to mealtime, he becomes filled up, and digestion has not yet fully taken place when it is time for the meal, he, of course, would refuse to eat. Be sure to give snacks further from mealtime; there should be at least two hours interval between the snack and mealtimes.

- **Taste disorders**. Your kid might be having a condition of taste disorder, which can change how some foods taste. A specialist (pediatrician) should be consulted ASAP.

Helping Parents

When we think "toddlers," what comes after is "play," especially when we are busy, maybe doing some house chore or the other, we never believe our toddlers can be of help. Parents need to learn to understand their kids (even though it's easier to say than to execute); we also need to understand that toddlers too, apart from tantrums and other displays of anger, can be serious at times. When they see us doing some things, they also want to try, but parents always think otherwise. Sometimes, when we even recognize their willingness to help, we simply refuse and tell them, "no, you'll get to help when you're bigger." We also just prefer to do these things by ourselves just because, if we allow them to do it, they end up messing it up; It is true toddlers aren't yet perfect at doing these things, but stopping them from trying doesn't help either. Allowing kids to help in house chores aids in their growth and development into adults.

Benefits

Below are some good returns of allowing toddlers to help with tasks.

- **Sense of belonging**: When kids get involved in doing the household chores, they get the feeling that they, too, are recognized as an important part of the family.

- **Confidence builder**: Being allowed to a part in the house chores make them know that you have trust in their abilities (no matter how tiny it might seem); this, therefore, gives them a level of confidence, which eventually becomes part and parcel of their personality.

- **Enhances their cooperation with others**: Working together with your toddlers in doing house chores helps build their collaboration and cooperation skills. Working with other people won't be hard for them since it's what they've been doing since toddler-age.

- **Promotes an appreciative spirit**: When kids get appreciated for helping, they grow to become appreciative beings, since you are their role model.

- **Builds self-discipline**: Self-discipline and responsibility-taking are also portrayed by kids who are involved in carrying out house chores.

However, with all these being listed, it's not all kids that want to help at all time, and getting them involved when they are not interested initially can be exhausting, but they can be left alone because toddlers need to be taught to help with house chores for their personality's sake, so some tips have been developed in order to get them to help.

Tips for getting toddlers to help

- **Not by force**: As I have always said, kids, like adults, never like being bossed around or dictated to; there is no room for dictatorship if you want to get them to help out with house chores or other things, let them decide they want to, when they are forced, there is a very high tendency for refusal.

- **Encourage collaborative work**: Do not make tasks like clothes folding personal; instead of asking them to fold their own clothes while you fold yours, you can just allow them to fold anyone.

- **Expect and allow the mess.** It is true that help from toddlers can make things a little slower, sloppier and messy, but you have to learn to allow for the mess to happen; although you will take care of it, it shouldn't be immediately, so as to not give your kid the wrong impression.

- **No task is too small**: Be sure to expose your kid to every possible chore, give a wide range of tasks from helping while sweeping, to helping out in the garden, to helping with laundry and dishes. Do not limit their exploration; try and make them redirect their energy usage from throwing things, hitting, and all that show of power, into using it for useful work for the family.

- **Sense of contribution**: The chores you let them do, of course, can't be "big," but be sure that the tiny ones they do are significantly important that it gives them the impression that they are truly contributing.

Kids also develop gross and fine motor skills when they carry out certain tasks (with parents' help, of course), involvement in chores also help sharpen Kids' brain, which helps improve their problem-solving skills.

Chapter 17: Parenting Requires Time. A Lot of It. And Patience, A Lot of It

Only when you have started to coach your emotions and be aware of them you can now coach their emotions; they need connection with you to self-regulate. Communicate your disappointment. Comment what is happening, take away the child that is crying, and then go back to the child that has misbehaved, connect by commenting what has happened, and acknowledge their feelings of frustration and anger as the base for their wrongdoings. Start from where your child is. Kids don't know they are doing the wrongdoing. No shame, no blame, but comment by repeating what has happened and try to acknowledge their feelings behind the bad action. Help them figure out what they can do to be better, express their emotions, accept emotions. You need to help your child to repair their actions; this later, we lead them self-regulate and motivated to take care of others and take better decisions.

Never withdraw love and affection.

Managing choice and freedom, power struggle, and the need for self-determination and free will in small children.

Effective Positive Parenting Tips

Positive parenting helps you make the best decisions for your child. There is no such thing as an ideal parent who is confident all the time, but you can learn specific tips to help guide your children with more confidence toward a better life in the future. If positive parenting techniques are not applied, then chances are the child will automatically be inclined to focus on the negative side of life.

Parenting strategies work when the child is in the process of growing, and the brain is developing. A child learns by observing first and then receiving an explanation verbally, so it is always better to portray positive parenting in your daily actions. In other words, live the life you want your children to have one day, and they will be much more likely to have a healthy and well-balanced childhood because of it.

Tips for Positive Parenting

Be the Model

Children need guidance and a figure they can look up to and admire. Be that person in your child's life by giving them a clear example to follow. For example, if you ask your child to throw their trash in the trash bin, then you have to do the same. Show them through action, and they will learn. Children look up to their parents and imitate their actions more than anyone else. They also watch their parents closely, even when the parent may not be aware, so be vigilant and conscious of your actions at all times. You have to be the person you want your child to be. If you show them a positive attitude, they will learn from it and do the same.

Be Loving

Know that love is something that can never spoil a child. Please show your appreciation through hugs, kisses, spending time together, talking about mutually exciting topics, listening to the music he/she likes, and much more. Love does not have to be mundane, just meaningful—anything that can create memories for a lifetime. Showing love for a child can help them develop a sense of calm and contentment. It introduces them to the emotional side of nature, which brings resilience and creates a close relationship with the parent.

Staying Positive

Try not to influence your child with your negativity, even if you hit with a challenge that brings out negative emotions. Rather than expressing negativity, try to think of ways to approach the situation with a positive attitude. Share your positive personality with your child so their brain learns to have positive thoughts no matter what the circumstance may be. Share positive experiences with them so they can have hope and goodwill.

Be There for the Child

Always be available for the child no matter what the problem is. Do not underestimate their ability to handle the situation on their own, but at the same time, always be the safest spot for them. Please support your child when they need you because it develops trust and closeness. Be responsive to a child because it directly affects their emotional development, and the outcomes of this approach are always positive.

Always Communicate

Make sure you keep small conversations on the go every day and recognize the importance of communication with your child. Do not miss a day without talking to them. Always listen to your child and speak to him/her carefully with understanding and respect for his/her perspective. Ask about any event which happened and listen to how he/she dealt with it. You do not have to impose your opinion but quietly listen to their view and acknowledge what they share. Please keep an open dialogue, so he/she can talk about anything without hesitation or fear. Excellent communication between a parent and child makes the child more cooperative and friendly as they grow up.

Change Your Parenting Style

Do not follow the same route your parents took with you to deal with your child. While your parents may have been great, there is always room for improvement, and what worked for you may not be as effective with your child. Observe positive parenting techniques and take notes on how you can do even better as a parent. Change your behavior positively, and you are bound to see a good result come of it gradually, if not immediately.

Maintain Your Well-Being

To implement positive parenting solutions, you must have things sorted out on your end. You need to pay attention to your relationship with your spouse and the things that you manage like your house and finances so that your brain is calm. Once you are relaxed and everything is fine on your end, then you are in a better position to raise a child to the best of your ability. If the relationship with your spouse is weak, then it will surely hurt the child directly or unintentionally. Take care of yourself in the best way you can, so you are at peace mentally and physically and can give your very best self to parenting.

Keep a Goal in Mind

How do you want your child to be when he/she grows up? Every parent has a dream that their child will possess a particular kind of behavior which the parent appreciates. Keep that goal in mind while you are raising your child. If you want your child to be positive, kind, helpful, and empathic, then show them how to be those things so they can follow by example. It's easy to lose sight of what you want for your child amid daily challenges. That's why it is so important to take a step back from time to time, look at the bigger picture, and re-adjust your approach with your long-term goal for your child in mind.

Never Stop Learning

Approach parenthood with an open mind. Acknowledge that is a job you can only aspire to master while the challenges in front of you will keep changing at every stage, and you need to adjust your priorities and values. Read about it and keep yourself in check!

Ways to Become a Positive Parent

So, by now, you're on board to becoming positive parenting. Keep in mind these fundamental principles as you go through your days with your kids.

I believe that if you intend to parent positively and keep in mind these eight overriding principles, you will have much more success.

Children need to feel like they have some control over their lives. "Instead of telling children what to do, find ways to involve them in decisions, and to draw out what they think and perceive." When we involve our kids in our day-to-day lives, they feel like they have more control and power over their worlds. Over time, this builds their self-esteem and ability to make choices on their own.

Kids need routines, and by getting them involved by helping to choose their methods, they get to understand the natural consequences of their choices. We do need to provide limited options, however, for our kids. It is through repetition and consistency that they will learn new skills. We need to create opportunities for them to grow and learn every day. By providing opportunities to help us throughout the day, our kids will learn what it takes to be a "grown-up." Kids revel in learning; for them, it is an exciting adventure. Don't make these learning opportunities away from your kids by scheduling and doing everything for them. Sometimes the learning is slow and messy, but that's okay. Get used to dirty and quiet.

Teach respect by being respectful

Listen to your children. Figure out what their needs are and respect their little personalities. Some kids need lots of breaks and quiet time during the day. Some kids thrive when there is a lot to do and want to play with other kids. Know your child and respect who they are. Respect their timelines, their needs, their schedules, and unique temperaments. Our kids are special and learn and move in the world on their terms. Celebrate that.

Use your sense of humor

Sometimes parenting seems like such serious business. You are serious about wanting the best for your children and giving them the best start in life. Kids are kids, and they need to not only feel safe, but they also need to have fun. A child's life should be full of fun moments and lots and lots of laughter. Sometimes we take our parenting role so seriously; we just forget to lighten up and laugh with our kids. It can be a lot easier to get our little ones to do something if we make a game of it and have a sense of humor when things go wrong. And things will go wrong.

Positive Discipline is not about giving your child everything that they want. Permissiveness doesn't help your child develop initiative or other social skills that they need. What you need to do, instead, is offer clearly defined choices and follow through on these choices with kindness and firmness. And, yes, you need to be consistent with your efforts. If you give them two options, don't let them make up a third choice. Make positive decisions are appropriate, not only for their age and development level, but also for their personalities. Again, we need to get to know and respect our little one's unique place in this world and start from there when we proceed into each day.

Be patient

We all know that kids are not our little programmable robots. And, we don't want them to be either. They come into this world with their temperaments, personalities, likes, and dislikes. They won't always agree with us, and as they get older, they want to do things their way more and more.

If we can truly empathize with our kids—see the world from their perspective, through their eyes—we will automatically be more patient with them. The world is a big, scary, yet awesomely fascinating place for a little one. They always told what they cannot do, what they should be doing, and how they should act. At times, this can become overwhelming for them, and until they can learn how to cope and self-regulate all of the time, there will be meltdowns. And I can't think of a time when our patience tested than during a meltdown.

Chapter 17: Parenting Requires Time. A Lot of It. And Patience, A Lot of It

Chapter 18: Peaceful Parenting: Mindfulness Tactics for Parental Stress Management

When working with or parenting a child, tween, or teen with any diagnosis, especially ADHD, we often undergo real feelings of immense pressures, marital strife, physical and mental health struggles, time and financial management, guilt, anger, sadness, loss, frustrations, stress, blame, and other adult challenges.

As mentioned, mindfulness is not a magical cure or pill to swallow, but it can certainly melt away stress and anxiety, like the Wicked Witch of the West was dissolved by the water in the movie. Once you master the basics and accrue practice over time, you will see the results in yourself and your kids! Experiment today with at least one of these Grateful 8 Strategies. They are not listed in any particular order of importance, so feel free to mix and match:

Under the Sea

Whether you are a wondrous water baby or a lovely landlubber parent, it is so necessary to deeply and truly connect with your inner parental mermaid/merman and maintain a parenting model that is not all about perfection.

Keep yourself afloat and your head above the waters. Recognize that like water freely flowing, parenting a child with ADHD is not stagnant and/or a perpetually picture-perfect or pretty pond.

Ride and let the waves and whirlpool of colorful emotions and evolving learning experiences exhilarate you and unveil your inner strengths amid the serious struggles (and sharks!). Do not forget to play and splish splash along with the way because humor will be your life vest as you surf steadily in life, teaching, coaching, and parenting!

Love Lingo

This technique is also imperative. Use your words, mindfully and compassionately. Do not fight fire with fire; do not allow words to become weapons when parenting kids, tweens, and teens with ADHD. Of course, this does not mean that you must speak in eloquent poetry and poise all the time, but learn love lingo.

Why? It can tenderly tame your tongue when we use love lingo instead. Following suggestions from Conscious Parenting experts, I have learned to take a moment literally since we as parents must really try and discern the difference between reacting to kids with ADHD from the central state of who they are and from our own proud, parental egotistical worlds.

While this advice might sound a bit harsh, love lingo roots us in reality and empathy, so it affirms that we as adults have already had our own time to grow up and learn the ropes of this world. Thus, love lingo is powerful because it reminds us not to make it all about us as the adults. What does this mean? It does not encourage you to be a pushover or a doormat, but try not to take everything, so personally, although I know it is much easier said than done.

It also forces us to stop comparing ourselves to other parents, the Kardashians, and everyone else out there. Who cares what others think about us as parents and people? Be authentic and live in love in your own skin! You are not in a pageant or parenting competition, so learn love lingo for confidence and empowerment.

One way to employ better love lingo is to have some handy dandy one-liners when tensions are high to diffuse your own adult egos. My favorite one, for example, is "I love you too much to argue." It works like a charm with my kids, spouse, and family members. What will be your love lingo line/lines be? Think creatively and practice, practice, practice. Live the love lingo when you are "Livin La Vida Loco!"

Pregnant Pause

No, this strategy is not advocating a plan to conceive another bun in the oven, foster an entire football team, or adopt triplets, but I assure you that it is one of the easiest ways to integrate mindfulness into your daily life routines and parenting approaches. Simply add a pregnant pause and breathe deeply when you feel overwhelmed, frazzled, angry, or ready to give up.

I love this idea so much that I actually suggest repeating it based on your age (or your kiddo's ages): so if you're 40, do it forty times! Words are so powerful, so "word up" with this holistic wisdom to cope with ADHD!

Slow Your Roll

Of course, you can order some yummy sushi when you are overly stressed
and over the parental edge, but this mindful strategy is equally imperative.

Kids with ADHD can become overwhelmed so easily and over-stimulated.
Don't let tons of back to back, crammed scheduled events, technologies, or
rushing around every day exacerbate the ADHD triggers? In turn, slow your
roll, ya'll! Take a minute and critically reflect upon this week's calendar. Talk
to your kiddos about which ones to prioritize. Discuss together ones to
possibly modify or delete in order to spend more face time with your kiddos,
not Facetime, the app. Slow your roll before stress takes a toll!

Balancing Act

Parenting in a mindful manner does not mean being a cop or being a lenient
buddy to kids 24/7. In actuality, it is truly about respectfully setting limits
and reinforcing your authority with "I'm the adult here" (Southgate, 2002, p.
210). It does not always feel this way when parenting, so this helpful tip is
one of my favorite pieces of advice for adults.

Similarly, the article, "Wonder Years," from Essence helps us to also realize
that as early as 9 months, we must model and reinforce to children
consistently which behaviors are acceptable and those that are not. If we are
constantly frazzled and depressed when dealing with a kids' diagnosis, then
we automatically model the negativity and toxic vibes that follow.

Think like a gymnast and find that proper balance; center yourself holistically and mindfully as a parent to keep your stress minimized and your confidence flying high amid ADHD!

Chillax

Taking a timeout is not just for kids. In reality, adults equitably need to take breaks in order to remain grounded and sane when parenting, coaching, mentoring, or treating kids with ADHD in any capacity or role. If your child is having a major meltdown, tantrum, diva session, or rebel without a cause chaos moment, I suggest using this technique on yourself called "Stop, breath, and chill" as (L., 2008) advises in "Peaceful Parenting" from Scholastic Parent and Child.

When attempting to take two sibling toddlers today to lunch at Panera Bread, sit with them on a small couch in the middle of a crowded mall while you are trying to order online, so you could skip the line and go straight to your table. Ask them to play calmly with their sticker together while you ordered. In less than 30 seconds, a circus ensued: they rambunctiously used the public couch as a trampoline, started pulling each other's hair, kicking, pinching, and sobbing loudly. You had to apply this technique to literally calm yourself first before attending to their mall mania. When do you need to chillax the most as a parent? What are you currently doing to distress less?

Pump It Up

Exercise is so essential and something that parents need to maintain mindfulness, health, and sanity. I know many experts recommend striving for roughly 10,000 steps per day, but my personal goal is 7500.

I swear I am not receiving any promotional or monetary compensation for suggesting them. They have literally toned and changed my life and mental health. They are also free and readily adaptable to suit any level, or need. Pump it up for parental patience and power in whatever way suits your style and preference.

Chapter 18: Peaceful Parenting: Mindfulness Tactics for Parental Stress Management

Chapter19: The Correct Way to Discipline a Child Based on Age

It doesn't matter how old your kid is. Each life part requires some teaching, and the discipline you give must be consistent.

Before starting the guideline, I want to tell you about the most important aspect you need to understand. If you, as a parent, don't stick to the rules and values that you set up, your children won't do it either.

But, let's take each period of your child's life of which you are fully responsible for mold and see what the correct ways to approach him or she is and how to teach them to become the best version of themselves.

Newborn to 2 Years Old

This is the time in which the babies discover the world, and with this discovery comes the curiosity and the desire to know more. During this period, the brain is exactly like a sponge that absorbs all the information surrounding them.

Because of this, the best thing you can do is eliminate attractions that can be dangerous, such as jewelry, medicine, or cleaning products, which can be ingested and produce harm. Also, I know that parents prefer leaving the child in front of a TV and do their house chores, but I highly advise the contrary. Video equipment at this age is just as toxic for the brain as chemical products are for the stomach.

Of course, crawling babies will tend to put their unacceptable hands-on objects. The simplest way to solve this is to simply but calmly say, "No." The worst thing you can do is to rush the child and yell at him or her. After gently saying, "No," try and distract the child with an appropriate activity. As I've said, at this age, they are really curious, so that a shiny suitable toy will captivate them, and they will forget about the forbidden gadget.

On the other hand, timeouts can also be a form of useful discipline for toddlers. Explain to your child how this kind of behavior is not acceptable and give him and her two minutes of a timeout to calm down. Always remember that you should not leave your child on their own during the time-out. You should stay with them, look at their eyes, connect and explain calmly why their behavior is not acceptable.

Whatever you do, don't spank your child. At this age, the child will not make the connection between the punishment and their actions. However, they will imitate you since you are their role-model and will tend to be even more offensive towards you and other kids.

From 3 to 5 Years Old

Your child is growing up very fast in this timeframe, and they start to understand more and more about life. Also, because during this interval, the child accumulates so much information, she or he will start making connections between their actions and the consequences that come from them. Due to this, it is the best time to start explaining the house rules.

So, it is important that you talk to your kid and explain the differences between right and wrong, how it is ok to behave, and what is forbidden.

For example, starting with the age of 3, whenever your child does something that you disagree with, such as throwing food on the floor; try not to yell. Remain calm and explain how wasting food is not acceptable in your house. Also, think of a suitable consequence for this action, like telling your kid that he or she does something like that, they will have to clean the mess.

The sooner you establish rules, the better it is for everybody. I know that sometimes it is always hard to express your dissatisfaction, but overlooking the violation of your own rules will not help your child grow up and turn into the person you want him or her to become. Empty threats will weaken your authority as a mother or father, and your kid will just test your limits.

The only thing that you should not forget about is that good deeds also have consequences, so be sure to offer your child a reward for every positive action. Tell your baby how proud you are of him or her with every occasion, but don't forget to specify the part of their behavior that satisfied you. By doing so, it is more probable for your child to repeat the gesture only to make you happy. This way, it will become a habit and will come to them naturally.

Of course, disciplining some kids will be an easier job than others. If you have a very stubborn kid with a very strong personality, you will need to try some other techniques. For example, give your kid a timeout whenever it does something bad. Be sure you send your kid to contemplate the things that have upset you, somewhere without distractions such as a TV or computer.

There is no exact time of how long the timeout should be. Try multiple time intervals and see what works for your child. Researchers say that for each year of life, you should add a minute, but again, you need to test and see what length is suitable for your case.

The last thing I want to talk about when it comes to disciplining a toddler is the necessity of giving clear commands, which are also self-explanatory when it comes to distinguishing right from wrong.

From 6 to 8 Years Old

This represents the period of time in which your child starts going to school and becomes more and more responsible for his life. Because of this, the education you give is very important, so let's see how you should act and how you shouldn't.

Even though your kid is older and knows more about what he or she likes or dislikes, it is still important to keep your rules standing and apply the necessary consequences.

Timeouts are still very effective, so don't be afraid to make use of them. One important thing is always to be consistent. It is very important that your child actually believes what you are saying. To be sure that your kid takes you seriously, don't start making unrealistic threats such as, "Do your homework, or you will not play PlayStation ever again in your life." Both of you know that this will not happen, so the child will just ignore you.

Lastly, remember that you are raising a child and not starting a military school. So, give your child not only the benefit of the doubt but also a second chance when he or she makes a mistake.

From 9 to 12 Years Old

You will notice that even though kids are growing up, it will not become easier to discipline them. However, if you follow the golden rule of natural consequences, then you should be able to educate your offspring without issues.

You will see that as they grow, they evolve and become more mature. With this, they will start requesting more freedom and trust. So, what you need to do is to teach them how to deal with the results of their behavior. By doing so, you will ensure an efficient and suitable method of discipline.

I propose to take an example and see exactly what I am talking about. Let's say that your kid has broken one of the school's windows, and you are called to the principal's office to discuss the issue. An inappropriate thing you can do is to rescue your kid from detention and not let him or her take the blame.

By letting your kid take the punishment, you will help him or her to learn a very important life lesson. They will learn that bad actions bring hard consequences, and even more importantly, they will acknowledge the fact that you, as a parent, won't always be there to save them.

Only by learning from their own mistakes, they will be able to keep themselves away from similar situations.

If you see that natural consequences don't have any effect on your child, remember that this age period is the best to use interdictions on electronic devices as a consequence of their actions.

Teenage Years

I consider this period to be the most difficult one because, during these years, your baby is no longer a child per se. They have their own desires and expectations and probably know what they want to do with their life. However, during these years, your child needs you just as much because they can make some very big mistakes that they will regret for the rest of their life. So, I advise you to pay great attention to what I have to say.

Until now, you already gave them the basis of the education they need in order to have a good life. Your kid is aware of what is good and what are the aspects of the life that should stay away from. Yet, they still need your rules and guardianship more than ever.

Therefore, set up boundaries even though most probably your child will hate them. Too much independence will not be good for your child, just as too much limitation will not prepare them for life.

This being said, let your kid have friends and go to parties, but be sure that those friends are not a bad influence, and curfew hours are set.

Don't forbid your child to date. It will just make them do it behind your back and do stupid things. Let them discover the meaning and implications of a relationship. Let your child know that you will always have an ear for their problems and a shoulder for him or her to cry on.

Most importantly, don't be afraid to talk about the sexual aspects of the life. This is exactly the age period when people are discovering their sexuality and become curious about their bodies. Talk to them about how starting their sex life is a very big deal and how they should wait for the right time and person. Explain to them the importance of protection and about the risks of contracting a disease or an unwanted pregnancy.

Even if your child will not feel very comfortable talking to you about these aspects, they need to know that you are open to discussion.

So, to wrap this part up, it is really important to establish the appropriate limits for your child at this age. The relationship you will have with your child will be influenced by this age period.

Last but not least, raising a teenager is not about control. It is about focusing on the positive aspects to help your kid discover their life path.

Chapter 20: The Common Mistakes That Parents Make and How to Fix Them

Disciplining your toddlers alone is not alone. You must also avoid the common pitfalls of parenting. Many of these blunders do not just decrease the effectiveness of the discipline that you impose on your toddler but may even encourage your toddlers to misbehave. Here are the common mistakes that many parents make when disciplining their children.

Being Aggressive

Some parents simply give up and become aggressive. The problem with being aggressive is that the children learn nothing except fear. They do not get to understand the value that you want them to learn. Instead, they obey you out of fear. Studies also show that toddlers who have experienced, aggressive or abusive parents are likely to grow aggressive as well. Being aggressive does not just mean spanking your kids, but it also includes using highly offensive words and threatening words. It is important to note that you are dealing with a toddler, and being aggressive is the worst thing you can do.

Comparing Yourself with Other Parents

Stop comparing yourself with other parents. How they discipline their kids is their problem. If one of your friends tells you that slapping your kid in the face is effective, even if he could prove it, do not follow the advice right away. After all, according to various studies, slapping or hitting your kids is not an effective way to discipline them.

Comparing your Child with Other Children

It is wrong to compare your child with other children, except if it will be something that will make him feel good about himself. Would you like your child to compare you in terms of money with a parent who is much richer than you are? Of course not. In the same way, you should not compare your child with other children. Your toddler is unique in his way, and you should appreciate him as he is.

Lying

Some parents lie to their toddlers to make them obey. Although this may work from time to time; it also has bad consequences. In a case study of a mom from New Jersey with a 2-year-old daughter, it so happened that one day when her child did not want to get in the car, she pointed at her neighbor's house nearby and told her kid that it was a daycare center full of troglodytes from a scary TV show. She told her daughter that she had two choices, to get in the car or be left alone in the house with a threat of being attacked by creepy cavemen. Of course, her daughter finally gave in and entered the car. Now, if you look at what happened, it will seem that it was successful. There was no shouting or spanking or anything that took place. However, the problem here occurred after the incident. Following the case study, the mom's daughter began to have a fear of daycare centers, thinking that such places have scary cavemen. As you can see, although the mother was able to make her child get into the car, the consequence was worse. Therefore, instead of lying, the best way is, to be honest, and be emphatic.

Yelling

You do not have to yell at your toddler just to get your point across. According to Dr. Alan Greene, a pediatrician and member of the clinical faculty at Stanford University School of Medicine, if you lose control and start yelling, your kid will also do the same. Now, this does not mean that your kid is intentionally disrespecting you. This only proves that your child is having a hard time with you because you cannot understand each other. Therefore, you must keep your voice quiet yet firm. Eye contact also helps.

Thinking that You Understand Your Toddler

The truth is that you cannot always understand your toddler. This is simply because toddlers do not think the same way as adults do. You simply cannot tell exactly how certain things have an impact on your toddler's feelings and thoughts. More importantly, you do not know just up to what degree. Therefore, do not be too hard on your toddler.

Raising the Child, you Want

Do not impose your life or your will upon your toddler. Your child has his own life. Let him pursue whatever he wants. Let him paint his dreams and believe in them. Focus on the child whom you already have and not the idea of a child in your mind whom you would wish to have. Your child may not be wired the way you would want him to be, and this is normal. Let your child have his chance in life. Let him believe and live his dreams.

Correcting Everything at the Same Time

Chapter 20: The Common Mistakes That Parents Make and How to Fix Them

Many parents try to correct all the inappropriate behaviors of their child, and they expect a toddler to be able to do it within a short period. This is a very unreasonable expectation. Even you cannot change your bad manners and behaviors quickly, so do not expect your toddler to be able to do it much more than you can. Not to mention, most parents' complaints about their toddlers are normal behaviors (or misbehaviors) for a toddler.

You must learn to pick your battles, and do not even attempt to win everything at the same time. You may start with the behavior that you consider to be the most serious and requires attention. Once you have corrected it, then you can move to another. Of course, you should discipline your child with every opportunity that presents itself. But, learn to focus on a particular behavior, so you can also gauge the effectiveness of the technique or techniques that you are using.

Long Explanations

Long explanations do not work on toddlers. You will only seem like talking gibberish after a few minutes. Do not forget that toddlers have a short attention span; therefore, long explanations do not work well with them. For example, you do not have to lecture your toddler why eating cookies before bedtime is not good for her teeth. She will learn that when the right time comes. Instead, just say, "No cookies." You do not have to explain so much. After all, toddlers are not meant to be very logical. They do not care so much about explanations. Of course, this rule is subject to exceptions, such as when the toddler himself wants to know the reason behind something or when giving an explanation appears to be the best course of action.

Bribe

Do not bribe your toddler just to make him do what you want. Otherwise, he will always ask for it, which could be a problem in the long run. In a case study of a mom in Montclair, New Jersey, she offered her daughter a piece of chocolate if she (her toddler) would eat her meal. It worked well. Her daughter finished her meal quickly. Up to this point, it would seem that bribing is also effective. However, what happened here was that after that dinner, the daughter would always ask her mother to give her a piece of chocolate so that she would finish her meal.

Instead of bribing your child, the suggested way is to help her realize the importance of food. Using the case as mentioned earlier study, the better way would be to tell her child that she will get hungry late in the evening if she eats so little and that she will not be healthy, which could make her sick. If you face a similar problem with your child, you can tell her about the health benefits of the food, like it could make her skin more beautiful, make her taller or smarter, and others—but do not lie.

Not Asking Questions

Toddlers usually have so many questions. As a parent, you tend to answer your question as much as you can. It is worth noting that you should not lie to your child when he asks questions. However, you can make silly answers, but be sure that he knows that it is a joke when you do so. Also, avoid giving creepy answers or those that will tend to scare your child. So, avoid answers that relate to ghosts and other scary stuff. However, parents get too caught up with answering their child's countless questions that they miss another important thing to do: to ask their child questions.

Chapter 20: The Common Mistakes That Parents Make and How to Fix Them

If you can take the time to ask your toddler questions, even crazy and illogical ones, you might just be surprised by the answers that you might hear. Toddlers have a powerful imagination and are very curious and open to almost everything. By asking questions to your child, you will also get to understand how he thinks, and even appreciate how young he truly is—so all the more reason why you should never be aggressive or harsh on your toddler.

Chapter21: Screen Time and Discipline

As already introduced at the beginning of this book, an old say states: 'it takes a village to raise a child.' Well, where is everybody gone? In today's modern world, more often than none people tend to leave away from immediate family members and old friends. Not everybody is surrounded by supportive communities with free baby groups or parks and play centers. No to talk about been locked in with your children during a pandemic! While home-schooling, continuing working, child-rearing, and housekeeping.

What about screen time? Some Parents feel guilty of giving any amount of screen time to their children. In a world of mostly full-time work, parents away from immediate family, and extremely expensive childcare. So, let's get a grip! Yes, all day tv is detrimental for your child/dren learning experience and often for the effects that tv can have on their behaviors. But it also is detrimental for your children to be around extremely tired, hungry, frustrated parents that are pressured from daily chores like preparing a healthy meal, pay bills, or answering emails.

Is there a chance for a happy middle?

Screen time should be treated like dessert plus try not to give their own screen, so you control them. Select contents, check the time, and so on.

It is difficult to stay happy and positive when stressed. You need to reconnect with yourself. Children won't develop self-control until 4 or later. So, this is your choice: reconnect with yourself, organize your home, control nap time and mealtime, and be happy. Or chaos.

There are so many things our kids do that can be regarded as a bad habit, but my focus is mainly on the one that affects modern kids the most, regardless of how he/she was brought up or what country they live in. Yep! You guessed it, their bad habits with technology. Every child today knows how to use a phone, the internet, computers, applications, and whatnot. One moment you are celebrating your child's first steps and words, then you blink, and they already know how to download a video game.

Ever since the inception of technology, parents, or should I say adults, in general, have been worried about how technology would impact their children—socially, academically, physiologically, and psychologically. These are all big words, but the bottom line is that there is a fear about how so much dependence on technology could affect our children's lives negatively.

These days, our kids are doing one thing or the other on the internet. The truth is, the internet is very addictive, and almost anything relevant to the social world these days is happening on the internet or on a screen. The question is, are you going to decide to cut off your kids completely from the use of technology, or look for ways in which we could use it to the advantage of our kids? I would recommend that we opt for the second option.

It may seem tricky and scary at times, but as a parent, you should not worry, because there are always old and new methods that can be applied for the children of today. Perhaps you have a long list of your worries and struggles (especially when it comes to technology and your kid using it), but in the following lines, you will read handy tips and information.

When your child is still young, it is quite easy to keep them under control towards everything, even for the use of technology. Doctors warn and parents worry that extended screen time can seriously affect a child's health (posture, sight, night rest, anxiety, excitement, aggression, and so on). Not all screen time is bad, and naturally, your child will want to watch cartoons or play their favorite game. Just bear in mind that screen time can be constructive, passive, or interactive.

Passive screen time is defined as spending time on a device (tablet or cell phone) or in front of a big (TV or computer) screen. Constructive screen time includes actual work and creating something new, such as web development, writing codes, designing websites, creating music (digital), drawing, and so on.

Passive time, as the name suggests, means watching a film, TV show, or a video. Interactive screen time involves playing video games, finding or downloading apps, and on-screen activities (sports or fitness).

Parents must be willing to control each type of screen time, because too much of anything is not good.

Here are a few tips for your child's screen time:

- Spend time talking to your children about their favorite online programs. Make sure it is not their only source of entertainment. Find a balance between their screen time and physical activities, play dates with their friends, learning, dining, and relaxation, but also creative and strategy games.

- Avoid commands because they usually never work. Pick nice words to encourage your kid to take breaks from their screen time. Once they realize that taking breaks in between watching TV feels nice for their eyes and entire body, they will willingly do it on their own.

Internet Access

The Internet is an upgrade in your child's technology life. The moment they get access to the network, they will realize that only the sky is the limit. No matter how useful and easily things can be found online, the Internet will make everything more challenging. At this point, every parent starts to worry about what their kids watch, read, play, and so on.

Video Games

I know you were probably thinking about it: "Oh yeah, Sandra plays games too much."

So, let me start with the positive aspects of gaming for your kids. Many types of research have been carried out concerning games, and many parents would like for it to be conclusive that all that video games do is make your kids anti-social. The results of the research have actually been the opposite of that; here are some of the advantages of letting your kids play games.

- Better hands and eyes coordination

A lot of games that your kids get to play could involve them having better coordination of their hands and eyes. By playing these sorts of video games, your kids will develop habits that are fundamental to helping them better their coordination as well as their puzzle-solving ability. The overall advantage of this is that they are able to easily solve complex problems when confronted with them in the real world.

- Higher cognitive function

Usually, it has been found that when something is done repeatedly for a long period of time, the brain works like the supercomputer that it is and finds a new way for it to perform those functions even faster. Basically, what the brain does is create new pathways and structures to help your child solve similar problems faster, and this also spills over to real life, of course.

- Health problems

It is true that too much of anything is detrimental, and this is true for video games too. One of the health issues that has been associated with playing video games is obesity. Due to the long hours spent sitting in one place and not doing any physical activity, your child can become prone to being obese. Another condition is the development of weak bones, weakened muscles, numb fingers, and weakened eyesight. All of these issues are prone to affect your child if he/she spends to0 many hours playing video games.

- Social isolation

Video games are mostly played indoors, and if your kid turns out to be a hermit in the first place or has a personality that makes him enjoy isolation instead of social mingling, playing video games might just be the right excuse that he or she needs to stay all day and all week indoors. The truth is that even without video games, a shy kid would still not prefer to interact with the outside world, but at least they can be more easily persuaded to go out and have some fun. However, with video games made available to them, trust me: there is no getting that kid out of the new Razer gaming chair you just bought for him/her.

- Declining academic results

Anything fun has a way of making itself seem more appealing than listening in class, doing homework, or studying for a test. Even just doing an activity like skipping rope after school can be more interesting than the impending doom of a test that your kid has to study for.

- Moral issues

Most of the games out there are geared towards teenagers and adolescents. This is because it is believed that at least a teenager is able to distinguish between what is right and wrong. However, kids who are still in their preadolescent ages might find it hard to distinguish between what is okay to do in a video game and what is not okay to do in the real world. This is where the choice of the kind of video games that parents allow their kids to play actually matters.

Tips for Growing Children with Mobile Devices

As your child grows, he or she will ask for a phone of their own. Everyone else has it, so they must have it too; you already know that story. This isn't bad per se; you would feel safer knowing that you could call them and ask where they are or if they need something. We are talking about the age when they are old enough to go to school alone, visit friends, have sleepovers, prepare simpler meals – you get the picture.

Part of today's kids' socializing is using social media.

So once your child (no matter if he or she is an adolescent) creates an account on social media, it is your responsibility to check what is going on there. Forbidding, it will not work, but, again, limiting the time spent on their phones can ease things up. If you see that they spend too much time using their social media and chatting with friends, you can easily pick an internet policy with limited mobile data.

Chapter 22: Nutrition

Mood Foods for Holistic Health

Similar to the sentiment expressed in Woolf's quote, mindfulness also targets this notion of mindful eating as a link to better holistic health.

Recent studies by (Yunus, 2019) from the renowned Exceptional Parent have asserted how there is a possible link between ADHD and high sugar, salt, and fat intake when kids receive diets with only minimal whole grains, fruits, and vegetables intakes (p. 24). Many findings specifically herald the benefits of a whole-food plant-based (WFPB) diet with minimal or no processing for protection against ADHD, cancers, heart disease, osteoporosis, and other chronic conditions (Yunus, 2019, p. 24) as well.

While I am not suggesting a rigid Biggest Loser style diet or any particular dietary model. I also want to arm you with research and resources, so you can explore and take it to the other level as far as what is best for your particular family's needs.

Are you ready for some yummy suggestions? Let us find those aprons, ok?

- **Snack Attacks**: Make snack attacks healthy with fresh fruits and veggies. Make healthy smoothies together with your child and add some chia and flax seeds to balance moods. MasterChef Junior, anyone?

- **Mr. and Ms. Clean**: This advice does not mean operating a pristine household free of dust bunnies and flawlessness, but it is about eating as clean as possible to avoid unnecessary additives and food colorings. Of course, kids are attracted to the colorful, marshmallow, vibrant products that are often so full of crap.

- **Diggity D**: There is "No Diggity" about it that Vitamin D is the superior sunlight vitamin that most kids, tweens, and teens often lack from excessive indoor gadget time, nutritional voids, etc. As a result, Laliberte's (2010) "Problem Solved: Winter Blues" from Prevention insists that we must all ensure that our family members are digging it with vitamin D proactively since it is closely linked to keeping our serotonin levels elevated and balanced (p. 48). This connection is something that is super important in kids, tweens, and teens with ADHD for critical brain balance and overall wellness.

Are you excited to dig it with D? Take a family hike, jog, stroll, or skate around the block. Find a local park and dive into the D!

- **Straight from the Hive**: Try warm milk with Manuka honey for a natural relaxer before bedtime with your kiddos. Other girls really love it on bananas with peanut butter and chia seeds, too. You can also add it to evening herbal teas to evoke some sweet dreams and deeper sleep.

As a slight disclaimer, because of honey's sugary contents, be sure to just use a small amount, roughly the size of a poker chip. Just do not try to karaoke Lady Gaga's "Poker Face" song, or you might lose face with older kids! BEE holistic, BEE well, and BEE wonderful when you try honey with your honey!

- **Sugar High**: As adults, we really need to embrace the "You are what you eat" mindset with all kids, but especially those who have ADHD. In turn, closely monitor sugar intake with their candies, sodas, caffeinated beverages, and all those ooey-gooey treats and desserts. Carefully monitor the amount of fast foods that you are serving to your families, no matter how tempting or timesaving it may seem. Studies encourage us to eat "clean" as clean as possible as opposed to relying on the fatty, greasy, over-processed foods. Clean eating will naturally "eliminate unnecessary food additives such as artificial colors, flavors, sweeteners, and preservatives that do not add nutritional value and may contribute to ADHD symptoms. Limit sugar intake to 10% of total calories daily (roughly 6 teaspoons for children aged 2 to 19 years)" (Rucklidge, Taylor, & Johnstone, 2018)

A female toddler recently attended a birthday party with tons of sugary cakes, candies, and fruity drinks. Then she began bitterly bickering in the car on the ride home to no avail from all the junk in the trunk (literally). Are you eager to crush that sugary rush and move toward mindful eating? You have been baking and cooking with dates as a natural sugar alternative when you make muffins and other goodies lately. While you are not a professional cook or baker by any means, you are encouraged to freely consult at the local library or online that focus on mindful and natural ingredients to curb those high sugar sensations that tend to exacerbate ADHD! Be mindful when dining out, and always looks for healthier family options.

Putting a freeze on fast food addictions can be so instrumental. (Valles, 1998) Pioneering article from Drug Store News also indicates how high sugar intakes can cause low blood sugar and chromium depletion. The fast-food frenzy is really taking a toll on our kids as "The average American now consumes an average of 152.5 pounds of sugar in a year. That large soft drink at the drive-through window contains roughly 22 to 27 teaspoonfuls of sugar. It is reported that increased sugar intake actually increases urinary chromium excretion. Over time, this could have an impact on behavior."

- **Move Over**: Dairy overload can often cause major digestive issues. When kids are literally plugged up, they can act out even more. To counter these tummy troubles, consider some new dairy alternatives like almond, soy, coconut, cashew, and oat milk. I also suggest adding probiotics to your kiddos' diets with more kefir, Greek yogurt, and other mood foods. In a toddler's case, they have been extremely helpful to tame tummies and boost moods. Let us Move over mindfully!

- **Veg Heads**: You can opt for a Meatless Monday approach for more mindful family eating. Try to replace traditional noodles with veggies such as asparagus, zucchini, carrots, etc. Indulge in Brussel sprouts, cauliflower pizza crust, corns, asparagus, etc. Be a vicious veg head and also add more veggies to morning egg dishes, especially omelets.

Make the Jolly Green Giant proud and be a veg head of household more often to facilitate holistic health and happiness in all kids, but especially ones with ADHD! Some toddler adores making and eating kale chips with me.

She has also recently been trying the freeze-dried snap peas, too. We never know what they will like until we experiment, right? Go beyond broccoli and green beans on your grocery run!

In essence, it is also highly advantageous to ensure that your kids, tweens, and teens are getting enough B vitamins in their diets: B1 is linked closely to many key functions like immunity, heart support, and mental processing; B2 offers energy, hair, skin, and eye health; B 3 stabilizes our memories, moods, and hearts; B5 can keep cholesterol levels in check; B6 is a sleep reliever. Are you ready for some "Sweet Dreams" by Queen Bye?

Finally, buzz with B-12 for increased mood and energy management. My young kids love the "classic ants on a log" snack with peanut butter, cashew butter, sunflower seed butter, or almond butter slathered onto celery with raisins, dried cherries, or cranberries.

- **Beanie**: While I am not talking about the cool, fashionable hats, try to eat more mindfully against ADHD with beans and legumes. Make black beans burritos, hummus with chick-peas, serve up some edamame, and add lentils or sunflower seeds to beam up your families' diets!

- **Magnesium Magnets**: Strive to add more magnesium into your family's overall dietary routines, especially in cases of ADHD. Studies describe how the average American is often highly deficient in magnesium "by about 70 mg daily. Magnesium is the calming mineral, since it is the principal mineral used to control the parasympathetic nervous system. There is also the potential for calcium deficiency. Many children complain of aching legs and will see positive results with the initiation of a well-formulated multiple mineral supplement" (La Valle, 1998, CP13.). Get your magnesium magnets via food or supplements today!

- **Finding Nemo**: Set a goal to serve a fatty fish to amp up those Omegas and vitamin D 2-3 times a week. Yunus (2019) reminds us of compelling research that depicts how those with ADHD may also have "lower levels of omega-3 fatty acids and higher levels of omega-6 that may lead to inflammation and oxidative stress."

Accordingly, Evidence by Rucklidge, Taylor, & Johnstone, (2018) also suggests that supplementation with omega-3s and/or a broad spectrum of micronutrients (for those not taking medication) may be beneficial for ADHD symptom reduction, but it is so important that all "Patients should consult with their primary care provider before starting any supplement and with a dietician before changing their diet" (p. 15). Get your rod and reel in some fishing action during family meals and snacks for more mindful eating.

In fact, salmon nuggets and fish sticks are always a major hit with the little one. Give it a try or more. They also can enjoy coconut shrimp with fun and tasty dipping sauces. How can you get your Nemo and Dory on and blast more fish in your weekly menus?

- **See for Yourself**: Fruits like pineapples, grapefruits, tomatoes, berries, mangoes, oranges, and kiwis, are a definite self-care saver for the blasts of vitamin C. I also recently discovered passion fruit, a rich source of beta-carotene and vitamin C, as recommended by the recent article aptly called "Mood Food" (DailyMail, 2019)

- **Zing with Zinc**: Assist your kids with ADHD in the culinary department to better zing against mood swings, common colds, flus, and other physical problems. Simply add more fruits and vegetables rich in zinc to their diets daily.

Chapter 23: Sleep Routine

Proven Strategies to Get Your Baby to Sleep through the Night and Get Some Good Sleep Yourself

As a toddler is learning, you need to introduce behaviors that he recognizes as being part of the going to bed process and a winding down of another day. Your toddler's body clock is not yet set, and all of the steps I have outlined will help you to help your toddler to establish those links. You can say that "Mr. Clock" says it's time to put the toys away, for example, so that the child does not feel that it's the parent's fault that the play has come to an end for the day. Here is the ideal schedule for putting toddlers to bed in ideal circumstances. Bear in mind that you will have to make adjustments when you are traveling when the child is not in his own home and at times of illness, but apart from that, the routine should become something the child becomes familiar with.

Toys Get Put Away

This is a good habit. It clears up the play area and leaves the house tidy. In some homes, this may be on the ground floor, and it's important what the house looks like. Invest in a huge toy box instead of expecting a child to sort through things and put them into certain cupboards as that may be a little difficult for the child to grasp. If you have drawing tools, these can all be placed into a plastic box so that they don't stain other things, but at the end of the day, all of the playthings are to be put into the box. Mom can help with the clearing up because toddlers love to mimic adults and will be happier to join in rather than be expected to do all of the work themselves.

Bath and Pajamas

This gets the child into the routine that he needs to be clean and relaxed at the end of the day. If you want to encourage your little ones to enjoy this time, invest in some floating toys and even bubble bath that is suitable for their delicate skin. This is a time when the child is preparing for what he knows lies ahead, and parents should supervise the bathing process and wash the child's hair. It can be a fun time, but don't make it too rowdy as you are also getting ready to wind down for the day.

Supper

It is known that kids who have supper, sleep better relating to this. You will see the kind of supper that is usually at this time of night. It is a light something just to stop hunger pangs and a drink but not too large. This is enough food for the night and will stop the child complaining about being hungry five minutes after being tucked in for the night. Supper should be a time spent sat down eating, rather than being active. If parents can sit down with the kids, this gives them the impression that they are not alone. After supper, make sure that one of you goes upstairs and draws the curtains to the nursery so that the bedroom ambiance is correct for sleeping. Check the bed and go back down to the children to encourage them to go to the bathroom and clean their teeth and have one last try at going to the toilet.

Tooth Brushing and Toilet

It's a very good idea to make sure that your little one has a clean diaper for the night, and this is the ideal time for that. Make sure that your toddler is encouraged to clean his teeth properly and to ready himself for bed. You may find that the child likes a little bit of independence, so I encourage parents to have a stool that the child can stand on. The more grown-up a child feels at this age, the more the child feels in control of learning things like potty training and hygiene, so encourage your child to enjoy this part of the evening.

Choosing Your Reading Material Together

You want to avoid any hurry at this stage. Take your time with your child and choose suitable reading material before placing the child into bed and tucking him in. The story should never be something that is going to wake him/her up but should be read in a low voice, so that the child can hear, but also so that he relaxes while the words are read to him. He may enjoy looking at the pictures, but at bedtime, make this kind of interaction minimal because you don't want to wake him up. You can promise him that you can look tomorrow at playtime, but make sure that you keep the promise as he/she will remember that you made it.

Getting The Room Ready For The Night

The room light should already be subdued, so when the reading is finished, tuck teddy into bed with your little one and ask him/her to look after teddy because teddy needs lots of love. Never skimp on a cuddle before you place the child into bed because, after the reading, all that is left is a little bit of affection and a goodnight kiss. The child knows that you are going to leave the room, and this may prove to be a difficult time with boys and girls. If it is, an extra cuddle won't go amiss, but the child does have to understand that bedtime is bedtime, and there is no negotiation.

Dealing with Crying

It is quite normal for a child to whimper before they go off to sleep. They are tired, probably a little grouchy, and now you are leaving them on their own in their bedroom, and that makes their little hearts a bit anxious. However, although you may be monitoring the sounds, be aware that this may die down very quickly if the child is left to it. Some systems have been devised whereby you are told by experts to ignore crying. However, if the crying gets too forceful, the child can get extremely distressed, and I would never recommend that to anyone. Go in and cuddle the child if you have to calm him, but remember that placing the child in his bed for sleep is very important. Any other reaction will encourage the child to keep on trying to win your favor when it comes to being moved into the grownup's bed.

You need to remember that psychological damage can come from fear and that this battle is about fear, not about wits. If your child is a little uncomfortable with the level of light, perhaps you can adjust the light a little so that he feels more comfortable. Sit on the chair beside the bed. Sing a lullaby if you want to, and you will notice that the child will gradually go to sleep. It may take a little bit of training, but the idea is that you gradually move away from the side of the bed. You are still there to reassure, but the distance between you should become more so that you can leave the room and carry on with your evening without too much problem.

Safety Considerations in the Bed Area

Make sure that the bed is not crowded in with toys and that there is nothing that can harm the child within the area of the bed. This should be a cozy place where the child can relax without turning over and hurting himself on sharp toys. You will know from the level of dribbles whether the child is teething, and this may give you a clue about the discomfort of the child. If you pop in before you go to bed and notice that the pillowcase is particularly wet, you can change it so that the wetness does not disturb your little one while he sleeps.

Catering for the Bodily Needs of a Toddler

On average, a toddler needs a total of 11 to 12 hours of sleep in 24 hours. Keep a diary note of the times that the child slept in the day, and you will get a much better idea of how to adjust the daytime schedule to encourage more tiredness at night. This will change as the child grows, but for the time being, it's important that you respect that need and that during the hours of being awake, the child eats food that is nutritious and gets plenty of outdoor exercises. This helps the child to get the most of healthy nutrition and fresh air, and all of this contributes to how well the toddler sleeps. A happy child who has a well-balanced life will be easier to train than one who is not given sufficient exercise and has excess energy to burn when it comes to bedtime. That excess energy could be the reason for lack of sleep, so adjust the daytime schedule accordingly.

Remember, there is no bargaining when it comes to bedtime. Many parents do barter with their children by saying, "Okay, one more story" or "Okay, you can come downstairs for another half hour" or by letting the child dictate the rules for bedtime. It has been proven time and time again that this isn't the end of the problem but is the beginning. A child who knows that a parent will bargain will be even more angry and upset when the parent decides that bargaining is not possible on certain nights of the week. Thus, you need to instill that just as a child eats his breakfast, he also needs to learn that certain actions are not negotiable. The ideal steps are ones that will get you off to a good start. Involve the toddler in every single step, including putting the toys away, sitting very still and quietly for his/her supper, going through the hygiene things like cleaning the teeth and going to the toilet, and the child will have a better understanding of what is to be expected at bedtime.

The things that will sidetrack you are:

- Illness and how to deal with it

- Crying that seems irrational

- Signs that something is wrong and getting to the bottom of it

- Insecurity was shown by the child in the way he/she acts out

Most of these are common sense things to deal with. For example, if you suspect illness, then a visit to the doctor can reassure you. Crying that seems irrational can be dealt with by sitting by the child's bed and trying to work out what it is that is upsetting the child, without taking the child out of the bedroom environment. Sometimes, the child just needs to settle down with teddy and have the reassurance that mom or dad is there listening to them. You can also go through the different areas of the room to reassure the child that there is nothing to be afraid of.

Chapter 24: Establishing Boundaries for Your Toddler

Make a Plan

You must be strategic and come up with plans about how you want to handle your toddler. As a parent, you must assume an active role instead of a passive role when it comes to parenting. You must always be a step ahead of your toddler. Well, the good news is that, as an adult, your prefrontal cortex is quite developed, unlike your little one. You are capable of strategizing and thinking rationally. Now, it is time to put these traits to good use. By paying little attention to your child's behavior, you will come up with various triggers or circumstances that cause your little one to fall apart. It might probably be a transitional activity like shifting from playtime to mealtime, or even a specific activity like bedtime. Spend some time and think about all these triggers. Once you are aware of his triggers, it becomes easier to deal with them. You can easily come up with certain limits well ahead and use them when the situation arises. It also helps you understand what your limits are, and the kind of behavior you expect from your child.

Mindful of Your Language

Whenever you are giving directions to your child or are setting limits, you must never use weak language. You must be firm and avoid using ambiguous words. Try to avoid using sentences like, "I don't think you should do that." Instead, you can say something like, "You must not do that!" or "You will be in trouble if you do that." Do you see the difference between these two sentences? Even if they convey the same meaning, the way you convey it matters a lot, especially while dealing with a toddler. If you want to become mindful of your language, here's a simple exercise you can try. The time you are conversing with your toddler, record it on video. When you have time, watch this video, and make a note of the language you use. If you notice any verbal habits you wish to break, then you can start working on them. Using wishy-washy language is a strict no-no. Using weak language will enable your child to think that he can test your limits. You must re-establish authority and make him understand that you are the leader of the pack, and he must follow you. Keep in mind that you are dealing with a toddler and not an adult, so the way you talk to him must be different from the way you converse with other adults.

Non-Verbal Communication

Non-verbal communication is as important as verbal communication. Most of the communication that takes place is usually through our body language and facial expressions. Therefore, it is quintessential that you start paying attention to these things whenever you communicate with your child. Non-verbal cues must never be ignored. If your words say one thing while your face says something else, you will only end up confusing your child. For instance, if you use a jovial tone while talking about any mistake a child makes, it will only confuse him. Never use a serious tone when you are praising your child. There are a time and a place for the different tones you use. Maintain a neutral facial expression and don't allow extreme anger to show on your face. After all, you are not trying to scare your toddler away now, are you? Don't use threatening body language and make yourself open. If you maintain a neutral facial expression, crouch down, and place yourself in close proximity to your child, you can effectively convey that you mean business. From a child's perspective, your presence is often huge and intimidating. So, get down to his level while explaining any limits or boundaries to him.

Your Tone Matters

Another aspect of non-verbal communication you must pay heed to is the tone you use. Always make sure that your tone is warm and welcoming, but firm. When you use a sharp tone, you will end up scaring your young child or even over stimulating him. When this happens, his flight or fight will be triggered, and his ability to understand you will dwindle drastically. Another trigger you must be aware of is yelling at your child. Never yell at your child while trying to discipline him. You can calmly explain any rules you wish to set without scaring him away. It is quite difficult to get a scared child to listen to you. He might comply momentarily but will get back to doing what he was doing once again. While setting boundaries, you must have long-term goals in mind and not just momentary compliance. If you don't want him to repeat any dismal behavior, then you must effectively convey the message to him. Don't startle and scare your child.

Immediate Compliance

Adults often have a tough time accepting a "no." So, expecting a child to comply with whatever you say without putting up a fight is not realistic. You must have a realistic view of your expectations while dealing with toddlers. Whenever you set a limit, establish a limit where it is a limit for you. Once you do this, then make sure that there is a little space left for feelings. It is highly unrealistic to expect a child to reply with an "okay, sure" when you say "no" to him. If you talk to him in a calm and reassuring tone, the chances of him understanding and respecting your "no" without putting up a fight will increase. If you don't want to give him another cookie, then say, "I said no more cookies. I know you want it, but you've had enough." By acknowledging the fact that he wanted something, and by denying it, you are helping him process his emotions. The only way to deal with and work through tough emotions is by handling disappointment. Have some faith in your little one and his ability to process his emotions. Keep yourself in check whenever you are dealing with your child's big emotions.

Reasonable Expectations

You must set certain expectations related to your child's behavior. As he grows, the way he behaves will change, so must your expectations. You cannot expect a one-year-old to behave the way a six-year-old does. For instance, a two-year-old might have a tough time-sharing his things with others without putting up a fight, whereas a five-year-old might find this quite sassy. A four-year-old might constantly ask you, "why?" whereas it is normal for a three-year-old to keep saying "no." Understand that as your child ages, he is developing—not just physically, but mentally and emotionally too. It is a lot to take in for him, and you must be happy that he is as pleasant as he often is! Dealing with change is overwhelming, and you must manage your expectations while dealing with your toddler. You must hold it all together and be his support system. Don't get frustrated with him if he doesn't behave the way you expect him to.

Decisiveness

You must always be decisive while setting limits and boundaries for your child. The slightest hint of indecisiveness will give your child the confidence to take you for granted. Even if you do change your mind about a decision, you must be decisive. It is not just about setting a rule, but you must be decisive while following that rule. Let us assume that you tell your child,

"You can watch TV for a while longer," on Monday because you are busy with some work, and then on Tuesday, you tell him, "You cannot watch TV today," because you are tired and want to sleep. You cannot change a rule according to your convenience. Being a parent is seldom about convenience. Remind yourself that you are doing something for the wellbeing of your child. Being consistent and decisive about a rule is almost as important as the rule itself. Children respond well to consistency. When your child knows how he is supposed to behave and what you expect from him, it becomes easier for him to act accordingly. If you keep changing the rules, you will only end up confusing him.

Using Humor

Humor is an effective tool that can diffuse tension and help convey your message easily. Using humor is a great parenting tool. You can start animating an inanimate object like a toothbrush or a rubber ducky and use a silly voice to convey your message. For instance, saying something like, "You better get dressed before I count to five," in a funny British accent will get your message across without scaring your child. A little humor every now and then helps lighten things up and motivate him to behave better.

Good behavior must come from within, you can teach it, but you cannot force him to behave like you want him to. If he starts doing something only because he fears punishment or because he knows he will be rewarded, then you are not teaching him good behavior. Fear of punishment and rewards might work for the time being, but you aren't teaching him the importance of good behavior by doing this.

Chapter25: Roles of Parents

The most powerful desire or drive in a man is often his physiological need to fulfill the act of procreation.

Modern society and families have changed drastically from generations. The new attitude towards sex (right or wrong) has led to an increase in the number of unplanned pregnancies.

Anyone can be a sperm-donor and be the biological father of a child, but it takes more to be a dad. It takes a lot more also to be a mom than carrying a child for nine months.

We often assume parenting should come automatically and that we will be better parents than the parents that raised us. Relationships are like rose gardens when well-kept. They are beautiful. But if we leave our relationships un-kept, we will end up with dysfunctional relationships that bring us nothing but stress.

Roles That a Parent Must Focus On

There are six main roles that a parent must focus on: Love, Guidance, Provision, Security, Friendship, and Development.

Each child is different, and some children need more attention than others, especially strong-willed children, but we must fulfill our role as parents regardless of the difficulty. One thing all parents must learn is that having children is undoubtedly a life-changing event.

No matter how many children we have, each child is different and unique with a different set of challenges.

Love

Some parents believe that loving a child will come easy, and for the most part, it does. However, there are moments when love becomes strained, and tempers flare. Maybe the child is not on your schedule and not allowing you to sleep (which happens the first few months of life).

Strong-willed children may often test the boundaries of love. They may often leave you exhausted and even depressed with their antics. If you are at your wit's end, you are not alone. The trick is to get help.

When you become challenged in raising a strong-willed child, try and get help. If you have a partner, you can both take turns in dealing with your difficult child. If you are a single parent, you may need to reach out for assistance in raising the child, from siblings or the grandparents, but don't try and do it alone.

Even when you are stressed-out from parenting, you still have a responsibility to love the child. If you start to feel the strain, seek help, and try to take a break if you can.

But when we talk about love in relationships, we are not just talking exclusively about some sense of mutual endearment or fondness.

Parenting a strong-willed child will require what is referred to as "tough love." As children learn about the world they live in, and they will often do make choices they shouldn't. As parents, if we love our children, then we must encourage them to do what's right. Sometimes we have a misplaced sense of what love is in parenting, and we focus too much on endearment in times when we are required to show tough love.

When we focus on being liked or loved by our children rather than on encouraging them to do what's right for their good, then it's not them that we love but ourselves.

You must ask yourself, are you sacrificing their long-term fulfillment and happiness in life for your short-term sense of peace and endearment.

When your child takes a jar of jam from the supermarket aisle and smashes it on the floor because you refused to buy a toy for them, what do you do?

However, you choose to correct the behavior is down to you, but you must correct this behavior. If we willingly allow them to develop a sense of self-entitlement and lack of respect for authority, we are not showing love, as we are facilitating and encouraging behavior that will prevent them from developing into well-rounded adults.

Some parents result in yelling to correct bad behavior. But shouting does not help at any stage during development. When tempers flare, and words are spouted out, there is no telling the damage those words can cause.

Sometimes it might be better to leave the child if possible and allow things to cool down, and for clear heads to prevail before dealing with the situation.

Many parents get upset with toddlers who simply don't know any better because they have not learned the difference between right and wrong. This lack of emotional control will only exacerbate the situation.

Love is the ability to look past mistakes and guide your kid regardless of the emotional toll of doing so.

Guidance

It is often said that the first five years are the most formative of a child's life. It is the parent's responsibility to teach them and build up the child emotionally. Praise the child when they have done a good deed and correct them when they have done something not so nice or pleasant.

Guidance is more than teaching extremes or polar ends of morality. Guidance is about helping them develop a moral compass, direction, and the noble traits and qualities we want them to have in life without indoctrinating them and stealing their ability to come to their conclusions.

A child does not understand the word "no," and unfortunately, that one particular word is the most familiar word a child will hear growing up.

During a child's exploration, a parent may look over to discover little Jane is digging in the dirt of a flowerpot. The mess, of course, is easy to fix, and the enjoyment of the soft squishy dirt between the fingers is new. However, it is the mess, not the action, that causes a resentful "NO!" from the parent. It is not as if the parent doesn't want Jane to play in the dirt; it is the mess she is causing.

The child may not see the difference in playing with this sandbox inside the house to playing with it outside. Yet, many parents may flare up and even spank the child as they lose emotional control. Understanding that your child does not understand the difference and taking the time to explain may be more beneficial than shouting at them in anger.

Many parent's sources of frustration stem from them repeating their bad parenting habits and expecting different results. Yelling and spanking are not always effective and can serve only to re-enforce your child's strong will.

In situations like above, it would be wiser to remove the child from the sandbox outside and explain the difference. Redirection is one form of guidance. Although it is simple to remove the child and explain the difference between the sandbox and the flowerpot, there will be times when it is not so easy.

Security

One of the most important roles of a parent is to provide security. As our children are developing, it is our duty not only to guide them but also to protect them from harm. There are many dangers in the world they are growing up, in particular, those brought about by the

Very choices our children may make.

But regardless of the source of danger, it is the parent's duty as a responsible adult to stand up for their child. If the child is bullied at school or if the child feels pinned against various odds, it is the parent's job to step up and fight for their child. Many parents these days leave the child to battle on their own with the mentality of the survival of the fittest. This mentality, however, may work in nature, but as humans, this concept is flawed. To build trust with a child, the parent must prove to the child that they will fight for them.

It is, however, the parent's responsibility to provide the child with a safe environment free from verbal, emotional, and physical abuse. Even if that does mean taking away a new phone so that the texts stop, or the computer, so the hate mail ends.

Friendship

Inwardly most parents desire to be best friends with their kids. At one point in their lives, we may have been the center of their world, but as time goes on, kids will often become disinterested in their parents.

This is why it is important where possible to foster friendship with our children at an early age. But friendship with our children should not be used as an emotional crutch if we are unfulfilled in our own lives.

Becoming friends with our kids is about fostering a loving relationship, where the child knows we are their parent, but still feels they can talk to us, hang out with us or share with us without always having the obstacle of the type defined role of parenthood.

New every day.

Mindful Parents go within and get quiet to access their power.

Mindful Parents practice presence, create their experience, embrace imperfection, and love themselves.

Mindful Parents are motivated, knowing that with every step they are changing things for the generations that follow.

I am a Mindful Parent.

Conclusion

Toddler discipline is not a negative concept, but one filled with the methods to teach your child how to cope, to use the left brain, and work quickly to stop the right-emotional mind from taking control. You learned twenty strategies, starting with child development knowledge and parental behavior through practical advice and examples to help you deal with specific situations.

Knowing when to discipline your child is very important, and it is essential that you take the time to examine your child before giving them a punishment. Are they just acting out, or is there a deeper reason why they are doing what they are doing?

Here are some times when you need to discipline your child:

When their actions put them in danger—If your child is walking up to a stove and you tell them not to, their instinct is to do it anyways. This could cause them to be injured, and this could put them in danger. The point of discipline is to help them to learn the difference between the right and wrong actions, and you should take steps to discipline if your child continues to do things that put them in danger.

When their actions put others in danger—If your child is covering the baby's face with a pillow, playing with matches around big sister and her long hair, or doing something else that could put someone else in danger, this is another time to punish. First, you have to explain to them why it is wrong, but once they have been warned, you need to follow up on the punishment to help them to avoid hurting others.

When their actions cause harm to someone or something—If they are running around the house, they can smash into something and break it or knock into you can cause you to drop the baby. When their actions have the potential to harm someone or something, it is important that you follow up on any promised discipline in order to help them realize how important it can be.

When they purposely do the opposite of what you tell them—If you tell your toddler, "Don't do this," and they immediately do it, that is direct disobedience, and they should be disciplined to help them learn to obey. It is important that they learn that obedience is essential, as it can help to save their life or prevent serious harm from coming to them or others.

It is important that you save discipline for the moments when it is really important, and that you don't just go around spanking or punishing your child because they act out. Make sure that the actions are extreme enough to warrant discipline, and that will help you to not spend all your time punishing your child.

You now have the tools in your box to be the parent your tot needs. You can start implementing all the strategies in the various situations when they arise, so you know you are raising a happy, healthy tot with confidence, responsibility, respect, and curiosity intact.

Remember the golden steps to listen, repeat, offer a solution, and correct the behavior over the long term rather than hoping one lesson will do. Your toddler is fantastic and deserves respect in everything you do, even if there are times when you need to use a kind-ignoring to reset the brain into a calmer one that listens to you as much as you listen to your toddler.

You have the power to shape your child or hurt your tot. Reading through the information and strategies, you must be the one to implement what you learned positively, even using reverse psychology to keep your child interested and learning. Whether you are looking to teach moral values, respect, good ways, or confidence, the tools are within these pages for you to continue referring to as needed.

Enjoy this time in your toddler's life, where anything and everything can be exciting, fun, and entertaining. As your child grows, they will calm down, stop getting into everything, but will still need your love and affection. Love and respect are the two things you should never withhold, even in the throes of upset.

Thank you, and good luck on your journey with your beautiful toddler.

References

DailyMail. (2019). Mood Food.

Hart, R., (2017). *Toddler Discipline*. La Vergne: Editorial Imagen LLC.

Hargis. Aubrey, n.d. *Toddler Discipline For Every Age And Stage*.

Hughes, E., n.d. *Smart Toddler Discipline*.

Laliberte. (2010). *Problem Solved: Winter Blues*.

L., F. (2008). *Scholastic Parent and Child*. LA.Montez, M., n.d. *Effective Toddler Discipline Methods*.

Rucklidge, Taylor, & Johnstone. (2018). *Effect of Micronutrients on Behavior and Mood in Adults With ADHD: Evidence From an 8-Week Open Label Trial With Natural Extension*.

Yunus. (2019). *ADHD*.

Valles, L. (1998). Fast-food addiction and anti-consumption behaviour.

CPSIA information can be obtained
at www.ICGtesting.com
Printed in the USA
LVHW051556121220
674004LV00013B/473